C0-AKQ-102

THE YOUNGEST

A COMEDY IN THREE ACTS

BY

PHILIP BARRY

NEW YORK
SAMUEL FRENCH
PUBLISHER
25 WEST 45TH STREET

LONDON
SAMUEL FRENCH, LTD.
26 SOUTHAMPTON STREET
STRAND

"THE YOUNGEST"

CHARACTERS

Charlotte Martin
Oliver Winslow
Mark Winslow
Augusta Winslow Martin
Alan Winslow
Martha ("Muff") Winslow
Richard Winslow
Nancy Blake
Katie

The action of the play takes place in a small New York State City.

Act I: *The living-room of the Winslows' house. Late June. (35 Minutes.)*
Act II: *The Porch. Fourth of July. (42 Minutes.)*
Act III: *The living-room, the following evening. (30 Minutes.)*

The following is a copy of the playbill of the first performance of "The Youngest," as produced at the Gaiety Theatre, New York, Monday, December 22, 1924.

ROBERT MILTON

Presents

"THE YOUNGEST"

A Comedy in Three Acts

BY

PHILIP BARRY

(*Directed by Robert Milton*)

THE CHARACTERS

CHARLOTTE WINSLOW	EFFIE SHANNON
OLIVER WINSLOW	PAUL HARVEY
MARK WINSLOW	ROBERT STRANGE
AUGUSTA WINSLOW MARTIN	VERREE TEASDALE
ALAN MARTIN	WALKER ELLIS
MARTHA ("MUFF") WINSLOW	KATHERINE ALEXANDER
RICHARD WINSLOW	HENRY HULL
NANCY BLAKE	GENEVIEVE TOBIN
KATIE	ALICE JOHN

SYNOPSIS OF SCENE

ACT I: *The living-room of the Winslow's house. Late June.* (35 *Minutes.*)
ACT II: *The Porch. Fourth of July.* (42 *Minutes.*)
ACT III: *The living-room, the following evening.* (30 *Minutes.*)

The action of the play takes place in a small New York State City.

THE YOUNGEST

See page 5

THE YOUNGEST

ACT I

SCENE: *The Winslows' living-room.*

TIME: *Late June. About six-thirty in the evening.*

DISCOVERED: CHARLOTTE WINSLOW *sits in a large armchair up* C., *working on a piece of filet lace. She is about 57, a slender, pink-and-white woman with very gray hair.*

AUGUSTA WINSLOW MARTIN *is lying on sofa* L.C. *head front, reading the "Atlantic Monthly." She is about 28, charmingly dressed, striking looking—a youthful replica of her mother, save for the rather sulky manner which takes the place of the older woman's querulous one.*

ALAN MARTIN *is sitting on chair above French window on* R. *(on the porch) reading a law book. He is 30—a tall, agreeable looking blond, well-dressed, well kept.*

MARTHA WINSLOW *(*MUFF*) is a cool, crisp girl of 23. She is sitting on stool at* R.C. *looking at a large picture scrap-book, which is on the table there.*

MARK WINSLOW *is standing at her* R. *looking on, has new straw hat in his hand, upon which he is arranging a bright colored band. He is 32, and dressed very carefully in white flannel trousers and blue coat.*

RICHARD WINSLOW *is sitting on bench at* L. *front of the table, back to the audience. He is about 22, and with a fresh, sensitive eager face. His hair has not been brushed since morning. He wears an old soft brushed jacket, the collar of which is turned up. His trousers are old gray homespun, pitifully out of press. His heavy brown shoes, once good, are now genuine antiques, and no attempt has been made to renew their youth by polishing. His white polo-shirt, with button-down collar, is badly frayed at the neck. His tie—an old, bright-colored figured foulard, is pulled askew. He is smoking a pipe and industriously writing with a pencil upon a large pad of paper.*

MRS. WINSLOW. Martha!

MARK. *(Is standing above* R. *of* T.R.C.*)* One of these little spoiled darlings, I suppose.

MUFF. *(Is sitting—stool,* R.C.*)* But that's not Nancy's fault. They go head over heels without a word of encouragement, don't they, Alan?

*(*MARK *busies himself with his hat standing* L. *of piano.* ALAN *is seated on chair on porch back of window* R. *reading a law-book.)*

ALAN. I guess you'll hold your own with her, Muff.

MUFF. I know my duty. When one has a guest, one effaces oneself. 'Gusta—she's coming! She's on her way now! Can you believe it?

AUGUSTA. She must need a rest badly, to spend ten days in this hole.

MUFF. *(To* MARK*)* Look—here she is the summer we left school— *(*MARK *again looks at the book.)*

MRS. WINSLOW. *(Is sitting arm chair up* C. *working on a piece of lace)* Martha——

AUGUSTA. You'll find there's some other reason than just a visit with dear Muffie.

MUFF. —And this was in the April "Spur"—at Miami.

MRS. WINSLOW. Martha——

AUGUSTA. —Otherwise she'd have asked you.

MUFF. Oh, dry up, will you?— The Lawrensons' dance, New Year's Eve. Isn't that costume amazing?

MARK. Not bad.

MUFF. She meant it to be.

MRS. WINSLOW. Mark——

MARK. *(Lays hat on piano, and goes to* MRS. WINSLOW*)* Yes, Mother——?

MRS. WINSLOW. If you can get your sister's attention . . . *(*MARK *to* L. *of* MUFF.*)*

MUFF. *(Simultaneously)*— Anita Paine's wedding-party at Lenox—and Nancy the only one who's not smiling. Who says she's not clever? *(*MARK *at* L. *of* MUFF *puts hands on her shoulders, turns her to* MRS. WINSLOW, *then crosses front of* R. *of table* R.C., *again takes up his hat.)* Oh—— Sorry, Mother . . .

MRS. WINSLOW. I simply want to remind you that Nancy's visit must not be a signal for a round of gayety.

AUGUSTA. "A round of gayety!" Here!—— *(*MARK *laughs, to* R. *of* W.T.*)* Isn't Mother sweet?

*(*RICHARD *commences thoughtfully to rap on table with pencil.* MUFF *turns away in disgust.)*

MRS. WINSLOW. Augusta, I'm afraid that since your marriage your ideas of pleasure have become something warped. *(*RICHARD *is tapping on the table with his pencil.)* Richard—you'll scratch that table.

(MARK *crosses to* U.R. *of sofa to see what* RICHARD *is doing.* RICHARD *stops.)*

MUFF. *(Back to the scrapbook)* Here's "The Times" account of her party. You were a fool to miss it. *(*RICHARD *lights his pipe.)*

MARK. *(At* U.R. *of sofa)* I can't be running down to New York for every little deb that comes out. *(*MARK *sniffs the air and looks at* RICHARD. ALAN *comes in to* U.L. *of piano)* Lord—if you've got to smoke a rotten pipe, why not try tobacco in it? *(Goes to window up* L. *and opens it.)*

MRS. WINSLOW. He mustn't inside, anyway. Richard——

MARK. *(At* U.L. *of sofa. To* ALAN*)* Have you fixed things with Lawson yet?

ALAN. *(At* U.L. *of piano)* No.

MRS. WINSLOW. Alan, I cannot understand why you make this very simple matter so—so monumental.

AUGUSTA. Honestly, you'd think Alan got paid for handling the family affairs.

MRS. WINSLOW. Well, doesn't he?

AUGUSTA. He does not. You all think that because he's my husband you can take the usual fees for granted, don't you?

ALAN. Never mind, Augusta. *(To* R. *of* U.T.*)* As it happens, Mother Winslow, the matter isn't so very simple.

MARK. Why isn't it? *(To above sofa.)*

ALAN. Lawson wants to resell the old house at Grand View. The purchaser requires some proof that you were sole owner.

*(*MUFF *rises, crosses front, sits* R. *of piano.)*

MARK. Well, why not give it to him, without all this hocus-pocus? *(*RICHARD *commences to whistle.)*

ALAN. *(At* R. *of work table)* Mark, if you'd

confine yourself to your business and leave mine to me—— (MARK *laughs at him.)*

MRS. WINSLOW. *Ah-ah-ah-ah-ah-ah!* Now, Alan——

*(*ALAN *goes out window up* R. *onto porch, returns to his reading.)*

AUGUSTA. *(Rising, rearranges pillows, this time for head up stage)* This place would get on any-one's nerves.

MRS. WINSLOW. Why, I don't see how you could ask for a more charming spot. Oliver has always said that——

AUGUSTA. Oliver! If Oliver took a fancy to Borneo, you'd think it Paradise. *(Lies again on sofa, head up stage.)*

MRS. WINSLOW. *(To* RICHARD, *who is whistling)* Hush! Richard.

MARK. Quiet!

AUGUSTA. Lucky Nancy. *(Softly as she stares into space)* Southampton, Lenox, Miami, New York.

MARK. *(At* U.L.*)* What's wrong with this?

AUGUSTA. Every day like the day before. Same people saying the same things.

MARK. Sounds dangerous, Alan! Only two years married, too.

AUGUSTA. That's one of the same things. *(*RICHARD *begins to sharpen a pencil noisily.* AUGUSTA *rises.)* Richard—for the love of Heaven! *(He stops, returns knife to pocket, and goes on writing.* AUGUSTA, *thoroughly irritated, stands for a moment biting her lip, then goes to bookshelves* U.L.C. OLIVER WINSLOW *comes in from the hall door at* R. *He has two newspapers in his hand and a third in the left pocket of his coat. Wears business suit.)*

OLIVER. *(Closing door)* Salutations, family!

AUGUSTA. Oliver—if you say that again!

OLIVER. *(Laughs)* Still in a temper? *(Through window to* ALAN. AUGUSTA *sits—chair at mantel, facing party* L., *continues reading.* MARK *hangs his hat on back of chair at* L. *of mantel.)* Better watch out, Alan—only two years, too! *(*MARK *and* OLIVER *laugh heartily. He goes to* R. *of* W.T., *takes* MRS. WINSLOW'S *hand, pats it.)* Well, young lady! How have you been?

MRS. WINSLOW. Dear boy—I thought surely you'd be home for luncheon. *(*ALAN *comes in above piano.)*

OLIVER. City Council Meeting. *(*OLIVER *goes to* L. *of piano and lays the two newspapers on it, takes a knife from his pocket and during the following lines cuts out a clipping about himself. To* ALAN*)* Old Lawson collared me again. Said he'd tried all morning to get you at the office. Weren't you there?

*(*MARK *hangs his hat on back of chair at* L. *of* M.*)*

ALAN. *(*U.R.*)* Why—uh—yes, I was there.

OLIVER. Then why didn't you give him what he wanted and get rid of him?

*(*MARK *crosses, takes a newspaper from* OLIVER'S *pocket and begins to read it, crossing to sofa—sits.* MUFF *crosses front of piano, taking one of* OLIVER'S *newspapers and sits on stool* R.C., *glancing through it.)*

ALAN. The—uh—the data isn't prepared yet.

MARK. "The data—" More hocus-pocus.

OLIVER. Why do you suppose I dug Father's will out for you?

*(*RICHARD *commences to destroy several sheets of*

his writing by rolling separate sheets into a ball, making quite a noise.)

ALAN. *(Comes down* R. *of piano)* Oliver, I think perhaps you'd better get another lawyer.

MRS. WINSLOW. Why, really, Alan, you——

OLIVER. *(Heavily)* Yes—I think perhaps we had. *(To* MARK*)* Have Luther Banks at the office Monday morning.

MARK. Yes.

ALAN. *(At* R. *of piano)* If you're so——

OLIVER. We needn't discuss it further. *(*ALAN *goes out window* U.R.*)*

MUFF. Noll! Nancy'll be here in no time. She's motoring from Cooperstown. Couldn't you just shout? *(*OLIVER *emits a faint Hurray!)*

OLIVER. I suppose we Winslows are having a great honor done us. *(To* RICHARD, *who is noisily destroying some of his papers)* Sh-h-h—don't do that. *(Cuts the clipping out of paper, then stands reading it.)*

MUFF. You'll think so, when you see her.

AUGUSTA. The Blakes are really very well-known in New York.

MARK. *(Is sitting upon sofa)* Oh, anyone with money can land at the top in New York— How about that notice for Miss Gracie's column? Did you say "guest" or "house guest"?

AUGUSTA. "Guest," of course.

MARK. Lord,—will you never learn?

MUFF. Listen, you two—get it into your heads that— *(*MARK *rattles his paper at her.)*

MRS. WINSLOW. Now, children! No wrangling! People are always speaking of what a devoted family we are, and——

MUFF. *(Smothered)* Aw!

AUGUSTA. *(Rising to* MRS. WINSLOW*)* What on

earth does it matter what people say? *(Goes to bookcase up* L.C.*)*

MARK. Well, will you listen to old Public Opinion herself?

MUFF. You're the one genuine, independent spirit, aren't you, Mark?

OLIVER. I think we all realize that a family's standing in its community is not a thing to be taken lightly.

*(*AUGUSTA *goes out window* U.L., *leans against* R. *side, continues her reading.)*

MRS. WINSLOW. We can always depend upon Oliver. I remember his father saying to me before he passed on: "Charlotte," he said, "even if I hadn't made the success I have, I shouldn't be afraid to leave you to Oliver." *(*OLIVER, *looking at clipping, is complacently listening. Others express, "Good Heavens, will we never hear the last of that story?"* OLIVER *goes to* R. *of* U.T.*)* "He's a brave little fellow, sincere, and strong-minded— He will be your mainstay." *(*MARK *turns his paper very impatiently.)*

OLIVER. *(At* R. *of* U.T., *chuckles, self-satisfied, pats her arm)* I simply happened to be the oldest, Mother.

MRS. WINSLOW. Dear boy!

MUFF. *(Looking through the paper)* Noll, while Nancy's here, I'll need some extra loose change—and the looser, the better.

OLIVER. *(To* MUFF*)* This is check day. Do you want to sign them, Mother? *(*AUGUSTA *to above sofa.)*

MRS. WINSLOW. No, Oliver—you do . . .

AUGUSTA. *(To* L.C. *up* L.C.*)* —Same old ritual. *(*OLIVER *glares at her.)*

OLIVER. *(Patronizingly to all)* I'll make them

out before dinner. *(Goes to piano—continues business with newspaper.)*

(A tiny Irish terrier puppy wanders into the room through the French window—up L. *goes toward* MUFF.*)*

MRS. WINSLOW. Oh—that animal again! Richard! *(*RICHARD *turns.)* It's very sweet, and we all love it—but it must stay outside. *(*RICHARD *crosses, picks up the puppy, hugs it and starts to take it out by window back* R.*—stops at* U.L. *of piano.* MARK *lights a cigarette.)*

AUGUSTA. *(Crossing to* F. *of work table. To* RICHARD*)* —And if that nasty little alligator comes under my door again—it's the last of it—hear? *(Re-crosses, as she passes* MARK *angrily fans the smoke away.* MARK *laughs at her. Goes to bookcase up* L.C. OLIVER *closes the window after* RICHARD *goes out. Comes to* L. *of piano.)*

OLIVER. Oh—uh—are you all— *(Looking about sees that window is open up* L.*)* Augusta, close that window. *(*AUGUSTA *closes window up* L.*)*—Are we all still agreed about Richard's allowance? *(There is a short silence.)*

MRS. WINSLOW. Yes—you are quite right, quite—

*(*OLIVER *crosses above sofa to above* R. *at* L.*)*

MARK. Absolutely! *(Rises, crosses.)* He won't go to work till he has to.

MUFF. *(Thoughtfully)* It seems pretty dirty to me.

*(*MARK *gestures with his paper to her—crosses to* L. *of piano.)*

OLIVER. It's for his own good, Muff. *(Sits chair above table* L. *and commences to make out his checks, uses his fountain-pen.)*

MRS. WINSLOW. *(Sighing)* Poor Richard.

MUFF. *(Rising—to* R. *of* W.T.*—tucks the paper under her arm)* Richard's all right. Chinese seems foolish, when you don't understand it. Not that I do— *(She takes a piece of candy from the box on the work table, bites it, exclaims with abhorrence, "Ough! Cocoanut!" Flings it into the fireplace, selects another piece.)*

OLIVER. Well, now, do you think— *(Sees* RICHARD, *stop.)*

*(*RICHARD *enters door* R. *with a manuscript bound in blue covers, and crosses front to sofa.* MARK *steps to* R. *of table* R.C. *and blows smoke in his face as he passes. For the most part he delivers his lines as if reading from a telegram. This unhappy mannerism is the result of trying for years to get a word in edgewise.* MARK *crosses to* L. *of sofa.)*

MRS. WINSLOW. *(As* RICHARD *is crossing)* Augusta—after the four solid, is it three in the air, or two?

AUGUSTA. H'm. *(Sits on upper arm of sofa.)* Four solid, skip one, two—in the air.

*(*MARK *sits on bench* L. *Suddenly* RICHARD *chuckles to himself.)*

MARK. Gather 'round—something amuses it. *(*RICHARD *disregards him.* MARK *quotes:)* "Don't sell the old house at Grand View. I used to go there as a child, and dream out my first stories." *(To the family)* He thinks people'll soon be coming to see where the great Richard Winslow first——

(Suddenly RICHARD *flips a pillow over his shoulder and into* MARK'S *face.)*

RICHARD. Damn you, Mark.

*(*MARK *rises, laughs, returns the pillow.* OLIVER *raps on table for quiet.* MARK *goes up* L., *crosses above to up* L. *of mantel. He takes a small pocket mirror from his pocket and rests it on top of standard. Smoothes down his hair, etc.* AUGUSTA *rises, comes down to above* DICK. MUFF, *angry, sits, chair* R. *of piano—reads her paper.)*

MRS. WINSLOW. Richard!

RICHARD. Well, if——

MRS. WINSLOW. I sometimes wonder if you will ever learn to control your temper.

RICHARD. If Mark'll let me alone——

AUGUSTA. *(To* RICHARD*)* That shirt is disgusting. Look, Mother—the collar's in rags. *(She plucks at one of the tattered edges.)*

MARK. *(At* L. *of mantel)* Bryon probably got himself up that way.

RICHARD. *(Scrunching away from her)* Oh—let it be. (OLIVER *turns and scrutinizes him.)*

OLIVER. Don't come to dinner like that. While Nancy's here, we'll dress.

*(*AUGUSTA *crosses front of sofa—sits on bench* L.*)*

MRS. WINSLOW. Oh, yes—and Richard——

RICHARD. What?

MRS. WINSLOW. I think it would be nice for you to take Mildred Spencer to the Club Dance tonight.

MUFF. *(Smothered)* Ha!

RICHARD. I don't.

AUGUSTA. *(Simultaneously)* Good idea, Mother. *(To* RICHARD.*)* Why not?

RICHARD. Not going. And if I were, t'wouldn't be with that unclaimed jewel. *(*MUFF *laughs.)*

MUFF. *(Is sitting chair* R. *of piano)* Score one for baby brother.

MRS. WINSLOW. Martha, that is not the sort of smartness to encourage. *(To* RICHARD*)* I told Mrs. Spencer that one of you would call for Mildred at nine.

RICHARD. Let Oliver.

OLIVER. I shall be with uh—Nancy. *(*MARK *glances at him quickly.)*

RICHARD. Let Mark, then.

MARK. *(Is glaring at* OLIVER, *turns to* MRS. WINSLOW*)* I shall be with Nancy. *(Sits chair at* L. *of* M.*)*

MUFF. If there's one thing she adores, it's competition.

RICHARD. Well, let me inform you that——

MRS. WINSLOW. This has gone far enough. You'll call at the Spencers' at five minutes before nine.

RICHARD. Well—if she tries to make me dance, I'll just break her leg.

MRS. WINSLOW. *(Raising brows)* That will do.

RICHARD. It ought to. *(*RICHARD *lays his pipe on lower arm of sofa.* AUGUSTA *tries to take it.* RICHARD *snatches it from her, then moves his seat to upper end of sofa, puts pipe in his mouth.)*

AUGUSTA. *(To* MUFF*)* Muff, where are you going to put her? Nancy, I mean——

MUFF. *(Hesitatingly)* —Richard's room, I suppose.

RICHARD. Oh, you aren't really going to make me move all my——?

MRS. WINSLOW. *(Placidly)* Katie went over it

this morning. You can go into the little room at the top of the stairs.

MARK. Hang it! That means using my bath.

MRS. WINSLOW. I don't think it will hurt you.

MARK. *(Rising)* Understand, youngster, I'll have none of your four-footed friends in my bathroom. *(Puts cigarette in ash tray on mantel.* RICHARD *stares at him impotently.)*

MRS. WINSLOW. *(To* RICHARD*)* Now run along, like a good boy, and change your things over.

RICHARD. Why's it always have to be my room? What's to prevent Noll and Mark from doubling up?

MARK. What with? Laughter? *(Pulls out* RICHARD'S *tie.)*

MUFF. *(Amused)* Can you arrange it with them?

RICHARD. *(Largely)* Can they arrange this with me?

OLIVER. *(With a wave of his hand)* Consider it arranged. *(*RICHARD *glares at him.)*

RICHARD. *(Rising—leaves manuscript on sofa, goes to* L. *of* MRS. WINSLOW*)* But Mother—you know I use mine twice as much's they do theirs. 'N all my books 'n papers are there——

*(*ALAN *enters* W.U.R., *goes to bookcase up* R.C., *changes law books.)*

MRS. WINSLOW. It will only be for a few weeks.

RICHARD. A few weeks! *(*MARK, *at* L. *of and behind him, takes* RICHARD'S *handkerchief from his pocket, loops it, throws it over his head to stop his talking.)* Mark! Let me alone! *(Removes handkerchief, puts it in pocket;* MARK *laughs—sits upper end of sofa. To* MRS. WINSLOW*)* Listen! Why do Alan and Augusta have to have two rooms? They're married—let them be domestic for a while. *(*ALAN *comes to* R. *of* W.T.*)*

AUGUSTA. You're not in the middle ages, my dear.

RICHARD. Don't see why you both stick 'round here, anyway. I know Alan'd be tickled to death to get away. But you—you've got to have your little luxuries, haven't you?

MRS. WINSLOW. When Alan and Augusta find a suitable home——

RICHARD. Yes! Came here from wedding-trip till they could find a house. Been plenty houses in last two years. Only not with tennis court, 'n swimming pool, 'n three cars, like this one. If I had my say your worries'd be over, Alan. Out she'd go tomorrow. In my opinion, she— *(*ALAN *sits chair at* R. *of mantel, reads his book.)*

AUGUSTA. The curious thing about your opinion is that it doesn't interest anyone.

OLIVER. *(Wearily, from the desk)* Oh, we know what room Nancy will have. Why discuss it?

RICHARD. *(At* R. *of sofa)* Exactly—no discussion— *(Takes key from his pocket and holds it up triumphantly.)* This key settles it. *(*MARK *rises and calmly picks the key from his fingers.)*

MARK. So it does.

RICHARD. Confound you, Mark! I'll— *(Tries to get the key, a little scuffle.* MUFF *rises, crosses above piano, comes down to above left of* RICHARD.*)*

MARK. Ah, ar, ar, ar! —Papa spank! *(*RICHARD *crosses—sits arm chair* R.*)*

MUFF. *(At* L. *of piano)* I'm sorry, Richard—but we can't very well show her into the coal-bin.

RICHARD. Sick of being treated like this! Who's she think she is, to come in here and take my room? Fool! I'll insult her! I'll act like the very devil!

OLIVER. We'll warn her about your—eccentricities.

MUFF. How I love people who make excuses for their families!

MRS. WINSLOW. I think this has gone far enough. Mark—let Richard into his room.

MARK. Yes, Mother— *(Crossing above piano.)* Come on—you of the lion heart. (RICHARD *does not stir, dangling the key in his face.)* —Are you coming?

MRS. WINSLOW. Then whatever you think should be moved, Mark.

MARK. Yes, Mother. *(Turns to go out.* AUGUSTA *rises to* R. *of sofa, picks up the Ms., looks about for a place to hide it.)*

RICHARD. *(Rising)* You dare touch my things! (MARK *laughs scornfully and goes out door* R. RICHARD *suddenly remembers his script, runs over to* AUGUSTA.) Augusta, give me that script. *(Takes it and runs out after* MARK. *Crosses above piano.)* Now, Mark, don't you touch my things. I'll do all the moving necessary. I've got some things there—— *(Exits door* R.; *closes door.)*

AUGUSTA. God bless our happy home. *(Sits sofa.)*

MUFF. *(To above stool* R.C.*)* It's sickening the way Mark rides him. He might let up for a minute, sometime.

OLIVER. Mark does go it pretty steadily.

MUFF. *(Swiftly)* You, too! You're about as light-headed with your darned helpfulness as—as a rock-crusher.

MRS. WINSLOW. Oliver knows what is best for him.

MUFF. *(Above stool)* Oliver is great. *(Throws out arms, chants it as "Praise be to Allah.")* Praise be to Oliver. *(To above piano.)*

MARK. *(Re-entering from door* R.*)* If ever anyone needed stiff treatment——

MUFF. *(At* R. *of piano—turning on him)* Mark, you do one more thing to Richard, and I'll kill you, see? *(She goes out French windows up* R.*)*

MARK. *(Calling after her)* Go douse your head, will you? *(Comes to* R. *of* W.T.*)*

MUFF. *(Off* R.*)* Shut up!

MRS. WINSLOW. Please! I don't want Nancy to get the impression that we are one of those constantly wrangling families. . . . (MARK *and* OLIVER *look at her. "Wrangling families"!)*

AUGUSTA. *(With a short laugh)* Mother!—as if anyone could!

(MUFF *re-enters hurriedly, from window up* R.*)*

MUFF. *(Breathlessly)* There's a car out front! She's here!

(Sound of doorbell off stage R. MUFF *runs out and closes door.* MARK *quickly crosses front of piano to* R. *of* W.T. OLIVER *rises—to upper* R. *of sofa.* ALAN *rises—to* L. *of piano.)*

MARK. *(At* R. *of* W.T.*)* Now the thing to do is to put her at her ease at once.

(MRS. WINSLOW, *rising, puts lace in work-box, takes up the box.* MARK *crosses to* C. *of mantel; arranges tie, etc., in mirror.)*

OLIVER. We'll make her one of the family, Mother.

MRS. WINSLOW. Yes.

ALAN. *(At* L. *of piano)* Oh, no! Don't do that!

MRS. WINSLOW. *(To* L. *of* ALAN) And why not, pray? I'm sure you haven't suffered from the—— *(Voices and laughter off right, followed by a loud barking. To above table* R.C.*)* Isn't that a—rather large sound, for the puppy? *(Lays the work-box on the table. Another bark.)*

THE YOUNGEST

See page 21

NANCY. *(Voice off* R.*)* Eustace! Behave! Remember you're visiting, you brute!

MRS. WINSLOW. Oh, dear——

ALAN. As I remember, she has rather a weakness for Great Danes. *(Crosses above piano to door* R.*)*

MRS. WINSLOW. Great Danes! Oh, haven't I enough to bear?

MUFF. *(Voice off* R.*)* Here, Katie—tell cook to feed him. *(Another loud barking.)* The bags go in Mr. Richard's room.

NANCY. *(Voice nearer)* In here?

MUFF. *(Voice off* R.*)* To the left, Angel——

ALAN. *(Opening door* R.*)* Here we are——

(NANCY BLAKE *enters door* R. ALAN *closes the door and stands with his back against it.* OLIVER *is front of* L. *of armchair* C. MARK *is at* R. *of* OLIVER. NANCY *is about twenty-one, slim, of medium height, strikingly pretty, and altogether charming in her knitted dress, bright tweed coat and straw hat, with its becoming "slouch." She is a kind of cultivated* MUFF, *more mature, surer of herself, with better manners and considerably more poise. She has been governessed, travelled and trained since she was old enough to walk, and she has taken on the best of it, and left the rest. She carries a small bag.* NANCY *goes at once to table* R.C. *and lays her bag down, then goes to* MRS. WINSLOW.)

NANCY. *(Going to her)* Mrs. Winslow!

MRS. WINSLOW. My dear—— *(They kiss.)*

NANCY. It was too sweet of you to let me come.

MRS. WINSLOW. Not at all. Are you feeling better, dear child?

NANCY. Like a girl again. What a pretty room! What nice-looking people in it! (MARK *and* OLIVER *step forward. She crosses to* AUGUSTA, *to* L.R. *of sofa.)* Augusta! It's been centuries! *(They kiss.)* How are you bearing up?

AUGUSTA. The sight of you almost revives me.

NANCY. If I had your looks, seven devils couldn't down me—— (MUFF *enters door* R. *The opening of the door throws* ALAN *up stage.* MUFF *crosses above* T.R.C. *to* NANCY. ALAN *crosses above piano and armchair* C. *and closes the door. Go to between chair and sofa.* AUGUSTA *crosses front—sits bench on* L. MRS. WINSLOW *sits stool* R.C.*)* Here, little Muffin—come and kiss your old Auntie—— *(They embrace; arms about each other, they face the family.* MUFF *is below* NANCY.) Honestly, Mrs. Winslow—you don't know what a joy it is to see this idiot again. *(A step up.)* Hello, Alan! *(Shakes hands.)*

ALAN. *(Is below* L. *of armchair)* Ah! you've recognized me.

NANCY. Two years, and not one wrinkle! You know, you and Augusta are upsetting the conventions of a confirmed spinster.

ALAN. Still confirmed?

NANCY. More so!—Muff—the brothers—quick! Which is which?

MUFF. *(Indicating)* Oliver—— (OLIVER *steps forward—shakes hands.)*

NANCY. How do you do, Oliver? (MUFF *sits upper end of sofa.)*

OLIVER. How do you do? We're so pleased that you've come just at this time. It's really the loveliest season of the year, for us.

NANCY. It seems perfect. I may settle here.

MUFF. —And Mark.

MARK. *(Steps in, above* OLIVER, *bowing low)* Delighted, I'm sure. We count ourselves most fortunate, to have such a charming house-guest.

NANCY. How like your pictures, Mark. *(To* MRS. WINSLOW*)* I'm afraid I brought my dog with me. Will you ever forgive me?

MRS. WINSLOW. *(Bravely)* We all love animals. Richard's pets have the run of the house.

NANCY. *(Crossing to sofa)* There! I knew there was a Richard! *(Sits below* MUFF.*)* Where do you hide him, Muff?

MUFF. *(Is sitting on sofa)* Oh—he's upstairs—

ALAN. *(At* U.R. *of sofa)* He'll probably be right down.

MARK. *(Below and* R. *of* ALAN*)* Sure—Richard'll be down. . . .

AUGUSTA. *(Sitting bench* L.*)* Any minute. . . .

MRS. WINSLOW. *(Sitting stool* R.C., *sighing)* Poor Richard! (NANCY *glances at her quickly.)*

NANCY. *(Slightly embarrassed)* Oh—uh—— hasn't he been well?

MUFF. Quite. It's just as I've always told you: they——

OLIVER. *(Below and* R. *of* MARK*)* He's a little odd, that's all.

MARK. *(Above* L. *of* OLIVER*)* You mustn't mind if he acts queerly when he first meets you.

OLIVER. It's just his way—quaint, you know. (OLIVER *and* MARK *laugh, embarrassed.)*

NANCY. I see. *(An uncomfortable pause.)* But I like quaint things. I'm forever collecting them.

MRS. WINSLOW. Oh—uh—is your dog a very large one?

NANCY. About the size of most bloodhounds. (OLIVER *and* MARK *look at each other, horrified.)*

MRS. WINSLOW. *(To* OLIVER*)* Bloodhounds!

NANCY. That's half their charm, being such a shock. *(To* MRS. WINSLOW*)* Mrs. Winslow, they're really the gentlest of all creatures. Eustace eats nothing but cereals.

MRS. WINSLOW. No? How—how interesting.

I—uh—I hope you're planning to spend some time with us?

NANCY. Till the Fourth, if I may.

MUFF. You try to get away that soon!

MRS. WINSLOW. Oh, yes—you must stay till after the—uh—the Fourth of July. It is quite an occasion for us. The townspeople always come up here at noon—out of respect of my husband's grandfather.

NANCY. *(Tenderly)* The dear old gentleman, he must enjoy that. *(*MUFF *whoops.)*

MRS. WINSLOW. Martha! *(To* NANCY, *gently)* He went to his reward in 1878.

NANCY. I beg your pardon.

MRS. WINSLOW. You didn't know.

OLIVER. —Out of respect to his memory.

NANCY. Of course.

ALAN. How about a swim before dinner, Nancy?

NANCY. I'm afraid the effect would be too—ah—superficial.

ALAN. *(Puzzled)* What?

NANCY. The dust on these roads of yours . . . ! *(She smiles.)* I want soap, hot water, and a very large scrubbing brush.

OLIVER. *(Laughs heartily)* Hah—hah! That's one on me! Isn't it, Mother?

ALAN. He's head of the Road Commission, big strapping boy that he is. *(To* U.L. *of sofa.)*

OLIVER. But, you see, with an average mean rainfall here of only one inch and three-eighths during the months of June, July and August, all roads are—— *(The family begin to show their boredom.)*

MARK. *(Interrupting)* We'd better be dressing.

OLIVER. Right! *(A step closer to* NANCY.*)* All roads are——

NANCY. It's after seven——

OLIVER. *(A step closer)* All roads are—— *(*MARK *to* R. *of* W.T.*)*

NANCY. Of course they are. What can one expect with such perfectly splendid mean rainfall?

OLIVER. Exactly.

ALAN. *(Going to window up* L.—*to* AUGUSTA) Come along, dear. There's time for a dive or two, anyway. *(At* W.U.L.—*to* OLIVER) Oh—do you want that will of your father's now?

OLIVER. Eh? No—send it to the safe-deposit. *(To* NANCY) All roads——

ALAN. I hope it doesn't give your new lawyer the shock it did me. *(Going out through the window.)* I think I'd stay in Richard's good graces a while if I were you.

OLIVER. *(Puzzled)* What's that?

MARK. It's after seven.

OLIVER. *(To* NANCY) As I was saying, all roads are——

(AUGUSTA *rises, starts up* R. *to follow.* RICHARD *enters from the hall, door on* R. *He does not see* NANCY. OLIVER *is standing in his line of vision.)*

RICHARD. *(To the family)* Well, it's all ready for her. *(Closing the door. All are trying to hush him.* MARK *to* L.L. *of piano.* MRS. WINSLOW *to* U.L. *of piano,* OLIVER *to* L. *of stool* R.C., AUGUSTA *to* L.L. *of sofa.* ALAN *returns, goes to* L. *of armchair* C.) But I'd suggest a lady's maid 'n some soft cushions 'n chocolates 'n cheap novels 'n——

MRS. WINSLOW. Richard!

RICHARD. *(At cabinet below door)* —'n maybe a couple of eunuchs at the door—(MUFF *rises, quickly)*—so that——

AUGUSTA. Of all the disgusting——

MARK. *(Simultaneously)* Look here, you——

OLIVER. *(Simultaneously)* That's enough!

RICHARD. *(Crossing front of piano to* L. *of*

MARK, *who is* L.L. *of piano—his voice rising)* —so that when your sap-headed little social celebrity arrives, she won't lose her sense of importance.

MRS. WINSLOW. *(To* NANCY, *with a nervous laugh)* Really, I——

OLIVER. Richard!

(RICHARD, *facing* MARK, *turns during the speech to* C.2. MUFF *is standing in* U.R. *of sofa.)*

RICHARD. Also, you might scatter a few butlers and footmen around, to impress her with—— *(Suddenly he sees* NANCY. *Their eyes meet. He stares at her for a moment, then turns sharply and goes out the French window up* L. ALAN *chuckles, then there is an awkward pause, broken by* NANCY.)

NANCY. Isn't he sweet?

MARK. *(At* L.L. *of spinet)* Yes, isn't he!

(OLIVER, *at* L. *of stool, crosses to* NANCY, *as if to explain, but thinks better of it, nods his head to her solemnly several times, and follows* RICHARD *out French windows, up* L. MARK *crosses to* NANCY.)

MARK. If you'll excuse us a moment—we have something to do. *(He follows* OLIVER *out window up* L. MRS. WINSLOW *crosses front of piano to* R. *of it.)*

AUGUSTA. *(Going up* L. *of table* L.) Dinner's at seven-thirty, you two. *(She goes out window up* L. ALAN *follows, exits window up* L.)

MRS. WINSLOW. *(At* R. *of piano)* I'm afraid we must apologize for my youngest son's lack of——

NANCY. *(Rises—goes to her)* Oh, no! Please!

MRS. WINSLOW. He is such a strange child. I—uh—I must see that your room's not all sixes and sevens. *(She goes out into hall door* R. MUFF *disgustedly flops herself down upon sofa.)*

MUFF. Lord! Again.

NANCY. *(At* L. *of piano)* Are they really on his neck every minute?

MUFF. Twice a minute. Half the time he's afraid to call his soul his own.

NANCY. Well, I call it rotten unfair. *(To* R. *of armchair* C., *looking at portrait over the mantel.)* Is that great-grandfather?

MUFF. So do I. What? Yes. Name's Jabez.

NANCY. Sweet name. I hate unfairness.

MUFF. You'll see plenty of it here, my precious. *(Rises to front of armchair* C.*)* Come along——

NANCY. Don't rush me. *(To* L. *of piano.)* I'm thinking—I suppose every big family has its victim . . . *(Takes off hat.)*

MUFF. Thanking your stars you're an only child?

NANCY. No—but people are so stupid! They don't realize that people actually turn out to be the sort of creatures they treat them as.

MUFF. *(Above* L. *of stool)* You don't really believe that.

NANCY. I do! Treat a mouse like a lion—he'll grow a mane over night.

MUFF. *(Crossing to front of piano)* Come on—let's dress.

NANCY. *(To* L.L. *of piano, taking off coat and hat and laying them on piano)* Take me, for intance: What if everyone hadn't always been so nice to me? I'd probably be a snivelling little idiot.

MUFF. *(Front of armchair* R.*)* —Instead of this choice confection we now behold—— *(Going to* NANCY*)* That's a pretty model—mind if I have it copied?

NANCY. Muff, I'm serious! *(A brief pause.)* But every now and then I get a streak of thinking— *(Sits stool* R.C.*)* It's sinful to be as happy as I am, without doing anything about the people who aren't. And when you wrote me about poor Richard cutting away from this only to be dragged back into it again —well, I did want to see you—but——

MUFF. *(At* L.L. *of piano)* Do you want six hundred nice pounds of family on your neck?

NANCY. Oh, I can manage them. *(Takes handkerchief from bag.)*

MUFF. Can you, though! You've got yourself in pretty deep before you know, with this Salvation stuff.

NANCY. *(Primly)* If you mean that wretched Maloney woman—that was all a misunderstanding.

MUFF. *(Ad lib.)* Oh. Yes—s——

NANCY. *(Rising, crosses to* L.R. *of sofa)* Now if you'll kindly produce the dear child.

MUFF. *(To above stool)* Nancy, do be sensible!

NANCY. I shall treat him as if he were the most important member of this family. Soon he'll believe he is—and at that moment he will be!

MUFF. Simple little formula, isn't it?

NANCY. *(Sits on lower arm of sofa)* In a few days I can make him over.

MUFF. *(To* C.2) But that's just what he hates!

NANCY. He won't know it's happening.

MUFF. Child! You haven't changed a particle.

NANCY. You don't think I can do it?

MUFF. No, I certainly do not.

NANCY. Any bets?

MUFF. Sure—anything you say.

NANCY. Ten dollars he'll be on top in a week.

MUFF. Make it twenty!

NANCY. Reckless infant—*(Snaps fingers)*—twenty it is.

MUFF. Done! Nancy—if you knew his family.

NANCY. Is it organized?

MUFF. Like a bank.

NANCY. Hasn't Richard any money of his own?

MUFF. Not a sou—beyond a tiny allowance.

NANCY. Money is important. *(A brief pause.)* —Did I say a week?

MUFF. (C.2) You did. Also—*(Snaps fingers)* —twenty dollars.

NANCY. *(Rising—to* MUFF) Then there's no time to lose. *(Turning her toward* R.) Go get him. Send him in to me.

MUFF. *(Turning to* NANCY) I'll do nothing of the sort.

NANCY. Alan, then.

MUFF. Nor Alan either. *(Takes* NANCY'S *hand; starts* R.) Now you come along if you want a scrub before dinner. (NANCY *releases her hand, then to above the stool.* MUFF *crosses front, takes* NANCY'S *coat and hat from lower end of piano.)*

NANCY. You take it for me.

MUFF. *(Opens door, stands leaning against the edge—looks at* NANCY *intently)* That once beautiful face of yours—really, I can't see it for dust.

NANCY. *(Gasps, crossing front of piano)* You're lying!

MUFF. It's just one huge black smudge. (NANCY *exits door* R. *Laughs and follows.)* Eau de Cologne—water'll never do it. *(Closes door.)*

(After a moment RICHARD *comes in the French window up* L. *with a tiny yellow and white kitten in his arms. He goes to* C.3, *looking about to see if anything is coming. Presently* NANCY *is heard off* R.)

NANCY. *(Off* R.) My bag— I'm sure I had it with me——

(RICHARD *goes to the* L. *of armchair up* C., *turns it a little toward* L., *the better to conceal himself, kneels, puts the kitten on the seat and commences playing with it.* NANCY *enters* R., *goes to table* R.C., *takes her bag without seeing* RICHARD, *and goes to door* R. RICHARD *has risen. He jumps to the door* R., *making quite a noise.* NANCY *is startled considerably.)*

NANCY. *(At the door, hand on the knob)* Oh, good grief! You shouldn't do that!

RICHARD. I—I can do what I like. *(Comes down* C.)

NANCY. Few of us are so fortunate.

RICHARD. N-N-N-Napoleon did what he l-l-l-liked.

NANCY. *(Still at door)* Ah, but look where he ended! *(Closes the door and comes to front of armchair* R.)

RICHARD. Wh—what does that—p—p—— *(He whistles)*—prove?

NANCY. *(To above the stool* R.C.) It's only a warning.

RICHARD. Humph!

NANCY. You're Richard, aren't you?

RICHARD. Who—s-s-said I w-w-wasn't?

NANCY. I'm Nancy Blake.

RICHARD. I n-n-n-n-n—know who you a-a-re.

NANCY. *(Thoughtfully)* You're not over-gracious to your guest.

RICHARD. M-m-maybe I sh-should fall down and w-w-worship.

NANCY. *(Interestedly)* Do you stutter all the time?

RICHARD. I can stop when I like.

(NANCY *laughs.* RICHARD *has the kitten in his arms. She extends her hand toward it.)*

NANCY. *(Going to him)* Oh—what an absorbing kitten!

RICHARD. Not a kitten.

NANCY. No?

RICHARD. Polar bear cub.

NANCY. Aw, let me hold it.

RICHARD. *(Turning away)* No, you don't! *(He crosses to French window* B.L. *and puts the kitten outside, then turns and looks at her.* NANCY *sits stool* R.C. *She smiles engagingly and finally he smiles in return. At window up* L.*)* They told you I was a little odd, didn't they? Well—I thought I'd be good and odd.

NANCY. *(Smiling)* It's your room I'm to have, isn't it?

RICHARD. *(Coming to* C.2) One of my rooms.

NANCY. I'm sure it's the favorite one. It's awfully generous of you. I admire generosity. I think it requires a truly great soul to be generous with anything so intimate as a room.

RICHARD. (C.2) Oh—er—that's—that's all right.

NANCY. I'm going to like you very much.

RICHARD. You're not so bad as I thought you'd be.

NANCY. You'll think better of me when I've had a bath.

RICHARD. There's a celluloid duck in the tub. Name's Millicent. Hold her under and then let her go. Sometimes she jumps two inches out of water.

NANCY. Oh—speaking of pets—— Does your dog object to dining with other dogs?

RICHARD. *(Delightedly)* You haven't got a *dog?*

NANCY. I've got six—but only one with me.

RICHARD. What make?

NANCY. Bloodhound. His name is Eustace.

RICHARD. Why?

NANCY. *I* don't know. Why's the duck's name Millicent?

RICHARD. *I* don't know, either.

NANCY. Well—there you are.

RICHARD. Where is he?

NANCY. Eustace? Kitchen, I think. *(He makes an involuntary movement toward door* L.*)* Would you rather see Eustace than me?

RICHARD. Much.

NANCY. You're awfully spoiled, aren't you?

RICHARD. Spoiled——? *(Returns to* C.2.)

NANCY. I suppose because you're a writer, the whole household revolves around *you.*

RICHARD. Ha!—— *(Goes to armchair* C.*)* They go along pretty much as they like.

NANCY. Yes! I've seen author's families before! But I like spoiled people. I'm one myself. You're the most interesting man I've met in a year.

RICHARD. *(Coming down* C.*)* You're all right, too.

NANCY. Thanks.—I do love flattery.—Oh, Muff said something about a dance at the Golf Club to-night . . . *(A slight pause.)* Would you condescend to take *me?*

RICHARD. Why—I—I've got to—that is—I've made other plans. (NANCY *eyes him whimsically.)*

NANCY. And, as usual, it's *your* plans that are important.

RICHARD. Why—if only——

NANCY. *(Rising,* R. *of* RICHARD) Oh, I shouldn't dream of upsetting anything so vital.

(ALAN *enters through the French windows up* L., L. *of armchair* C. NANCY *to* L. *of piano.)*

ALAN. *(To* RICHARD) Noll called down to me he's got a letter for you to post.

RICHARD. I guess it can wait.

ALAN. He said he wanted it mailed right away.

RICHARD. Well, he can——

ALAN. Better step, son—better step. (RICHARD *hesitates a moment, then crosses above piano.)*

RICHARD. *(Uncertainly)* I'll—uh—I'll see if it's important—— *(To door* R.*)* It may be important. *(To* NANCY*)* 'Scuse me. *(She smiles. He goes out door* R.*)*

NANCY. *(At* L. *of piano)* Does he always do what he's told, like that?

ALAN. Sooner or later. Has to.

NANCY. *(To* L. *of armchair* R.*)* Alan, we two know each other pretty well, don't we? *(Sits on the arm.)*

ALAN. *(Smiling)* We sailed boats together in Central Park.

NANCY. Then surely we needn't bother with preliminaries now. I need help. Will you promise to help me?

ALAN. *(*L. *of stool)* Why, of course. What's the——?

NANCY. It's just that I can't go merrily along and let a sweet boy like Richard endure the torment he does.

ALAN. Oh—— *(A pause.)* If you don't mind my saying so, I think there are enough people mixing in Richard's destiny already.

NANCY. In the wrong way, yes. *I* shall——

ALAN. It's the interference itself he resents. I'd let him be, Nancy.

NANCY. Before I leave, he'll be on top of the lot of them.

ALAN. A pleasant little task you've set yourself.

NANCY. I can't stay long, so there's no time to fool with half measures. I want a downright blow-up as quickly as possible. Can you suggest a way to get it?

ALAN. *(Sits—stool* R.C.*)* One occurs here on an average of twice a day.

NANCY. I mean a real one. Can't we trot out the family skeleton?

ALAN. I don't think there is one.

NANCY. How absurd! We have three. Blackmail! I've always had great faith in blackmail. Oliver's old enough for a past. Has he one?

ALAN. Like a prayer-book.

NANCY. They make me sick—— *(A pause.)* How about his father's will?

ALAN. What do you know about that?

NANCY. Only what I heard you say to what's-his-name—Oliver. *(*ALAN *studies her a moment.)*

ALAN. Well, there's nothing up *that* alley.

NANCY. There isn't?

ALAN. Not a thing. Honestly, Nancy. I advise you not to fool with this family. It's loaded.

NANCY. Then there *is* something up that alley! *What,* Alan?

ALAN. Well—uh——

NANCY. Stupid! Don't take so long!

ALAN. Well, in clearing the title to some property Mrs. Winslow sold, I discovered that her husband's will was made some eleven months before Richard was born.

NANCY. *(Eagerly)* Could he break it, then? Of course! Oh, marvelous, Alan.

ALAN. You don't know anything about it. As a matter of fact, he wouldn't *have* to break it.

NANCY. Oh, you *lovely* man! *Why* wouldn't he?

ALAN. Although everything was left outright to the widow, the New York State statute says a child born after a will is made inherits just as if there hadn't been any will.

NANCY. Then he'd *get* something? Oh, I'm shaking all over. Alan—— *(He looks at her inquiringly. She shakes her head decisively.)* I want a clear week to see what kindness and understanding will do. Then, if we need this—— *(Referring to the will.)* —It's awfully nice to know we have it.

ALAN. *(Rising)* But my dear girl, I tell you—

NANCY. *(Rising)* "But, but, but!"—Alan, you promised!

ALAN. But I didn't expect——

NANCY. But you promised unconditionally!

ALAN. All right—only I've an idea that some day you're going to get in a little *too* deep, young lady.

NANCY. *(Eagerly)* *Will* there be tight corners to get out of, do you think? Splendid! There's nothing like them on earth, to keep you thin. (AUGUSTA *comes in from hall door* R., *dressed for dinner. She has a newspaper in her hand for the roses.* NANCY *hastily goes out past her.)* I shan't be a minute, really!

AUGUSTA. *(At* R. *of piano)* Don't hurry me! *(She removes flowers from the vase on the piano, putting them in the newspaper, ready to throw out.)*

ALAN. *(*L. *of piano)* Darling—seriously—don't you think we've stood these family rows long enough?

AUGUSTA. *(*R. *of piano)* We'll look for a house again next week. You know there isn't a thing we can afford anywhere close by.

ALAN. Then let's go across the river.

AUGUSTA. But, my dear—that's the wrong side of town!

ALAN. Well, what of it?

AUGUSTA. Things like that are important, here.

ALAN. *Less* important, perhaps, than—— *(He stops as* RICHARD *enters from the porch window up* R. ALAN *goes to* L. *of mantel.* RICHARD *wears his hat and is smoking his pipe. When he sees* AUGUSTA *he flings his hat on* W.T. *and crosses eagerly to her.)*

RICHARD. *(At* U.L. *of piano)* 'Gusta!—What do you say to this as an idea for a story—a novel, maybe! *(Unconcernedly, she wraps the dead flowers in a newspaper.)* —There's a girl who's always had everything she wants. *You'd* call her spoiled, I suppose. But in *her* case it's——

AUGUSTA. Tell me when I've had something to eat, will you? *(She goes to French window up* R. RICHARD *follows her.)* Don't *bother* me! . . .

(AUGUSTA *exits window up* R. *with flowers. She leaves the flowers outside on the porch and crosses on the porch to window up* L. OLIVER *has entered door* R. *He is dressed for dinner. He crosses front of piano to above table* L. *Tears off first check for himself—puts it in pocket. Note: Checks are already written in; he only has to sign them.* MARK, *in dinner clothes, follows* OLIVER *in. He goes to upper* R. *of piano and grabs the pipe out of* RICHARD'S *mouth.)*

MARK. Don't you know that's forbidden in here? *(Crossing above* RICHARD *to front of armchair* C., *looks about for a place to throw it.)* Why aren't you dressed?

RICHARD. *(Picks up the empty vase on the piano)* You give me that pipe, or I'll just simply drown you! (ALAN, *to get away from the squabble, crosses above the armchair* C. *and exits window up right.* MARK *has stopped in front of armchair* C. *at* RICHARD'S *threatening attitude; stares at him uncertainly.)* Give it here. (MARK *lays the pipe on the* W.T. *and takes* RICHARD'S *hat there; throws it at chair at* R. *of mantel.* RICHARD *takes up his pipe.)* I'll smoke where I like, and I'll dress *as* I like, see? *(Replaces the vase on the piano.)*

MARK. Someone's been feeding him meat. (RICHARD *goes on smoking.)*

(AUGUSTA *enters window up* L.; *stays there a moment.* MUFF, *in evening clothes, enters door* R., *goes to above the piano.* MRS. WINSLOW, *also in evening clothes, follows* MUFF *in, crosses front of piano and to stool* R.C. *Sits.)*

OLIVER. *(As he tears out the check)* Here's your check, Muff. *(He tears off the checks one at a time as he gives them out.)*

(AUGUSTA *goes to* L. *of table* L. *for hers.* MUFF *crosses above* RICHARD; *goes to upper* R. *of sofa.* RICHARD *crosses above the piano, sits, and commences to run his fingers over the keys.)*

MUFF. *(At upper* R. *of sofa)* Oh, thanks, Noll. *(She looks at it.)* Wheeee! You're a brick. *(She crosses front of sofa and sits on bench front of the table.)*

OLIVER. Don't thank me. Thank Mother. *(He crosses above the sofa to* MRS. WINSLOW *and gives her a check.)* Here you are, you young spendthrift.

MRS. WINSLOW. Thank you, dear boy!

OLIVER. Don't you give it away, now. *(*MRS. WINSLOW *puts the check in her work-box on table* R.C. OLIVER *returns to above table* L.*)* Richard——

(RICHARD *crosses to upper* R. *of sofa.* OLIVER *gives him a check.* RICHARD *turns to* R.C.4. MARK *steps in to upper* R. *of sofa for his.* OLIVER *gives* AUGUSTA *hers—she is at* L. *of table.* OLIVER *gives* MARK *his.* MARK *goes up toward* L. *of mantel. They murmur "Thanks" or "Thanks very much."* RICHARD *at* C.4, *examining his, looks first surprised, and then dismayed.)*

RICHARD. *(To* U.R. *of sofa)* Look here, Oliver—

this is wrong. It's only *half*—— (AUGUSTA *above, watching* RICHARD.)

OLIVER. We have decided that you must be limited to this until you are more amenable to our ideas of what is best for you.

(RICHARD *looks at the faces around him, one at a time. Only* MARK, *who is up near* L. *of mantel, and* AUGUSTA, *who is above the sofa, meet his gaze.* MRS. WINSLOW *looks away.* MUFF *turns away.* AUGUSTA *continues crossing; sits armchair* C.)

RICHARD. *(Sits upper end of sofa—slowly)* —Call this a rotten deal—very rotten——

OLIVER. It's for your own good.

RICHARD. Everything disagreeable that's done to me is.

MARK. *(Has taken out his handkerchief and is repeatedly folding it and trying it in his breast pocket to get the best effect)* It's about time you learned that to have money you must earn it, as we do.

RICHARD. *You* earn your *allowance?*

OLIVER. Mark and I draw very nominal salaries, as a matter of policy. What mother gives us is to make up the difference. I've told you that time and again.

RICHARD. No—that's why you've always got so much *more* than me.

MRS. WINSLOW. *(Mildly)* But Richard——

MARK. You've been out of college for nearly a year without doing a stroke of work.

RICHARD. Put in eight to ten hours a day writing 'n studying. What do you call that?

MARK. A child could write your sort of stuff.

RICHARD. Is that so? Maybe *you* could?

MARK. With ease, my boy.

OLIVER. How much has it paid you?

THE YOUNGEST

See page 38.

RICHARD. *(With infinite scorn)* Oh—*money*—

MARK. *(Putting handkerchief in pocket)* What's money to we artists? *(Takes final look in mirror, then puts it in pocket.)*

RICHARD. 'Bout what grammar is to you pin-makers! *(To* OLIVER*)* Pins!—Why should I go into the pin business with you? Wouldn't care if I never *saw* another pin.

MUFF. Well, a good old pin *might* make your pants hang better, darling.

AUGUSTA. You know Mother offered to put you through Law School.

RICHARD. That's what *she* wants. I want to write!

MARK. Everything you've ever written has been returned.

RICHARD. Well, it takes time, just like everything else does.

OLIVER. Too *much* time.

MRS. WINSLOW. When Oliver was your age he had been in business four years.

RICHARD. Yes—and done what? Lost more'n a third of all Father left!

MARK. Noll was a very young man at the time.

OLIVER. —And there happened to be a panic.

MRS. WINSLOW. He had to learn how to manage in such crises.

RICHARD. He had to learn his *business!* So do I!

MARK. He calls writing a business.

OLIVER. Oh, let him rave.

RICHARD. Can't you even *understand* a person *wanting* to be anything but a big frog in this little puddle?

MARK. Our baby is ambitious.

RICHARD. I hate people who keep trying to make other people over. Conceited, meddling busybodies. Think you're doing it out of kindness, don't you?

Well, you're doing it just to make your own sweet selves feel more important.

AUGUSTA. Grateful for the pains we've taken over him, isn't he?

RICHARD. *(Crosses to her)* Mother—for twenty-two years now I've been treated like a hunk of putty——

OLIVER. Oh, I guess you haven't been treated so badly. You've got a good job offered you. Do your writing in the evenings. What do you say? *(*RICHARD *turns to piano. A pause.)*

RICHARD. *(To above stool* R.C.*)* Suppose it was the other way 'round? Suppose you two wanted to make pins 'n I wanted you to write. What if I said, "Make your pins in the evenings." *(*MARK *and* OLIVER *look at each other and laugh.)*

OLIVER. Don't be ridiculous.

RICHARD. *(Crossing to sofa)* You'd see, quick enough, how——

OLIVER. *Don't be ridiculous! (Murmurs)* How silly—make pins in the evening.

RICHARD. *(Sits sofa—slowly)* I'll—I'll go off somewhere by myself——

AUGUSTA. —And worry Mother sick again, eh?

RICHARD. It's *you* who worried her sick with all your lies—telling her I was starving 'n' all that. I'd have managed—if you hadn't come after me with all your soft talk 'n' promises 'n' reproaches about breaking her heart——

MRS. WINSLOW. *(Rising—to above* RICHARD*)* Richard, I——

RICHARD. *(Takes her hand)* I'm sorry, Mother—but you don't know—you just don't know. *(To* OLIVER*)* You shouldn't do this. *(Rises, crosses to stool* R.C. MRS. WINSLOW *sits sofa.)* I've got a right to be what I want to be—and I *could* be, too, if you'd all just let me alone—— *(He looks away,*

THE YOUNGEST

See page 42

his eyes glistening. Sits stool R.C.*)* Oh, if only you'd let me *alone!*

MARK. Well, it's nothing to weep over.

RICHARD. If I wanted to be disagreeable the whole time, like *you* are, I wouldn't have to stand it—— (MARK *groans, "Oh, don't be silly!"* OLIVER *smiles indulgently.)* I tell you I wouldn't.

OLIVER. *(Good-naturedly)* Then—if you're so oppressed—why on earth don't you be? *(There is a pause.* RICHARD *looks directly at him, then a spasm of pain crosses his face. He bites his lips and drops his head.)*

RICHARD. *(Barely audible)* Because I—don't want to be—see?

MARK. *(Sits chair at* L. *of mantel)* Ho! Ho! Ho! Pretty thin—pret-ty thin!

MRS. WINSLOW. Please, children, please! What will Nancy think?

MUFF. *(Rising to* R. *of* MARK*—to* OLIVER *and* MARK) Which of you'll take her to the dance to-night? I want the other for myself. . . .

(ALAN *enters* W.V.R. MARK *and* OLIVER *look inquiringly at each other.* MARK*, crosses to* U.R. *of sofa, takes a coin from his pocket, catches it on back of his hand and covers it with other hand.)*

OLIVER. *(Rising)* Tails. (MARK *uncovers the coin.* OLIVER *looks at it and laughs.)* Too bad! (MUFF *attempts to snatch the coin.* MARK *takes it from her.)*

MRS. WINSLOW. I'd rather it were Oliver. He's the oldest; and people will expect——

MUFF. It *is* Oliver, Mother. *(Crosses to* L. *of spinet.)*

OLIVER. Rather pleasant, sauntering into the ballroom with such a stunning importation. *(Sits above table* L.*)*

RICHARD. *(Is sitting stool* R.C.*)* You'll look even more like a pompous old dowager.

MARK. *(To* C.3) Hush, hush, Dickie-bird—you mustn't say naughty things, or Mildred won't like you. . . .

RICHARD. *(Disgustedly)* Mildred! (MARK *laughs.)*

(NANCY, *in evening clothes, enters door* R.*)*

NANCY. *(To front of armchair* R.*)* Of course, I'm not *late*. . . . (MRS. WINSLOW *rises—above stool* R.C. MARK *to* L.R. *of sofa.* OLIVER *rises and crosses above sofa to below* L. *of armchair* C.*)*

OLIVER. Not at all. (RICHARD *rises and crosses up to window up* L. NANCY *to* R. *of* T.R.C., *watching* DICK.)

NANCY. Oh—that's *good* of you . . .

AUGUSTA. We were just discussing the dance to-night. (NANCY, *still watching* DICK, *moves toward* R. *of* W.T.*)*

OLIVER. *(Below* L. *of armchair* C.*—nodding)* —And we're very anxious to have you see the Club. They say there's nothing finer, even on Long Island.

NANCY. *(Below* R. *of* W.T.*)* I'm sure there's not.

MARK. *(At* U.R. *of sofa)* At least there *won't* be —with *you* there.

NANCY. I think you'll be a great comfort, Mark. (ALAN B.C. *up* R.C. *At* R. *of* W.T., *crossing to* R. *of sofa.)* Hi, Richard . . .

RICHARD. *(To* L. *of table* L*)* 'Lo, Nancy . . .

NANCY. Millicent wouldn't jump worth a hoot. *(All look at her, puzzled.)*

RICHARD. You need deeper water.

MARK. *(Above and* R. *of* NANCY) Oh—you've met——

THE YOUNGEST

See page 42

NANCY. Very informally.

(KATIE *enters from the dining-room, door on* L., *comes to above sofa.)*

(WARN Curtain.)

KATIE. *(To* MRS. WINSLOW) Dinner is served, Ma'am. *(She goes out door* L. *and there is a general movement toward the dining-room, led by* MRS. WINSLOW.)

MRS. WINSLOW. Dinner is served, children. *(She crosses to* L.L. *of sofa.* MUFF *is near* L. *of piano.* NANCY *is at* L.R. *of sofa.* AUGUSTA *rises, goes to above sofa.* MARK *to* U.R. *of sofa.* ALAN *is at* B.C. *up* R.C. RICHARD *is* L. *of table* L.*)*

OLIVER. *(*C.B*—to* NANCY) Speaking of tonight, the lucky toss of a coin gives me the honor of taking you to——

RICHARD. *(Interrupting quickly)* Oh, by the way, Nancy—I can manage about this evening all right.

NANCY. *(At* R. *of sofa)* —But the other plans—that you said were so—vital?

RICHARD. *(Snaps his finger—largely)* Let 'em go.

OLIVER. I was saying, I'm to have the honor of taking you to the dance tonight.

NANCY. That's awfully nice—but would you believe it?—I've already promised Richard.

(RICHARD *chuckles.* MUFF *throws out her arms in joy.* OLIVER *stares and* MARK *scowls at* RICHARD.)

MRS. WINSLOW. *(At* L.L. *of sofa—to* NANCY) But—but——

NANCY. *(At* L.R. *of sofa)* You hadn't made different arrangements, Mrs. Winslow?

MRS. WINSLOW. Why—uh——

MUFF. *(To* L. *of stool* R.C.*—quickly)* Oh, no,—of course not.

MRS. WINSLOW. No, indeed—no, indeed. *(To* MARK *and* OLIVER*)* Then one of you will have to take Mildred.

OLIVER *and* MARK. *(Together)* Yes, Mother—

*(*RICHARD *laughs lightly. All but* NANCY, MUFF *and* ALAN *glare at him.* MRS. WINSLOW *exits door* L. *to dining-room.* AUGUSTA *follows.* ALAN *crosses above sofa and follows;* MUFF, *laughing, crosses above* OLIVER, *slaps him on shoulder, goes to* NANCY, *takes her hand and they start for the door; as they pass the bench,* MUFF *drops* NANCY'S *hand and, preceding her, stands at upper side of door as* NANCY *goes out.* MUFF *follows.* OLIVER *and* MARK *go last.* RICHARD *brings up the rear.)*

RICHARD. *(At* L. *of* T.*)* Lucky Mildred. *(*MARK *and* OLIVER *turn on him.)* Won't she be pleased, though! *(Then solemnly)* But I like this spirit of friendly competition, boys. *(*OLIVER *and* MARK *start for the dining-room.* OLIVER *crosses below sofa.* MARK *crosses above sofa.* RICHARD *makes way for* MARK *to pass him by, coming into above* L. *of table.)* All I can say is: may the best man—*(He pats them on the back simultaneously as they pass through the door, one with his right hand, the other with his left)*—win. *(He follows them into the dining-room as——)*

CURTAIN FALLS

THE YOUNGEST

See page 45

ACT II

AT RISE: NANCY, *in a morning dress, is seated in the swing, deep in thought.* ALAN'S *coat is over a chair* L. *After a moment* MUFF *enters from French window* L., *with a large piece of toast in her mouth, a coffee-cup perilously balanced in one hand, and a leather case of manicuring implements under her arm.*

MUFF. *(To* NANCY*)* Bless the girl! I thought you were still asleep. *(Sits chair above table* L.C.*)*

NANCY. I am practically—where's the family—all out decorating?

MUFF. If you mean Richard, he's still in bed.

NANCY. That sounds like progress, doesn't it?

MUFF. More like a collapse from exhaustion.

NANCY. We've been in before two every night. Two's not so wicked.

MUFF. —Not with Mark or Noll, with Richard it's plain dissolute. Agh! This coffee's been made for hours—— *(She opens her manicuring case and begins to file her nails.)*

NANCY. *(Simultaneously)* Poor lamb! It's the first chance he's ever had to get a word in edgewise.

MUFF. Lot of good it'll do him.

NANCY. Oh, Muff, he does *need* kindness so!

*(*MARK *enters from the house, window up* L., *carrying four campchairs. He regards* MUFF'S *manicuring implements with abhorrence.)*

MARK. *(At* L. *of* H.*)* I think that occupation is best confined to the boudoir.

MUFF. *(So sweetly)* The hell you say. *(She continues to file.)*

MARK. *(L. of hammock)* Good morning, Nancy.

NANCY. Good morning.

MARK. *I* call this a day, don't you?

NANCY. Heavenly. Doesn't it make you just want to be kind to everyone? *(MUFF chuckles knowingly.)*

MARK. It certainly does. *(Turns L. MARK glances significantly at MUFF, and receives an aggravating smile in return.)*

NANCY. *(Sighing)* I wish someone would be to *me*—

MARK. *(To L. of H.)* What?

NANCY. —If only I had someone to turn to—— But there's no one—no one.

MUFF. Poor girl. *(MARK scowls at her, then, softly, to NANCY.)*

MARK. *I* have the honor of being at your service always.

NANCY. I need help *so* much——

MARK. *(To front of L. of H.)* Try to tell me—— *(Rests two chairs on the H.)*

MUFF. "Give me but a word—a sign"! *(MARK opens his mouth to retort, then decides that the best method with MUFF is one of cold disregard.)*

NANCY. I—I suppose it *is* rather indirectly, though.

MARK. *(Sits L. side of H.)* That doesn't matter.

NANCY. Doesn't it?

MARK. Not a bit.

NANCY. *(Slowly)* I—suppose—the *real* need—would appear to be—Richard's. . . .

MARK. *(Chilling)* Oh! *(Rising, picks up the chair, front of L. of H. MUFF laughs.)*

NANCY. You see?— It has to be entirely personal. *(She throws up her hands.)* Oh, men—!—Men!

MARK. *(Protesting)* But I didn't say I wouldn't. . . .

NANCY. *(Cynically)* Thanks just the same, Mark.

MARK. Now really—what have I said?

NANCY. *(Softening)* Well—I *was* going to ask you if you'd mind being kind to Richard for the next few days. . . .

MARK. Why, really, I wasn't aware that I——

NANCY. *(Quickly)* I know. *I* meant to make a point of being more than usually so,—whatever he does, or however irritating he may be. Richard is in trouble, Mark.

MARK. *(Almost a whisper)* What's he done?——

NANCY. The trouble is more—uh—mental.

MARK. *(Disappointed)* Oh!

NANCY. He is an exceedingly sensitive boy on the brink of a great transition in his life.

MARK. You mean getting his crazy writing-bee out of his bonnet?

NANCY. —I hardly know. But he needs helping hands— My little hand . . . *(She looks at the lovely, helpless thing and drops it into her lap, with a sad, wistful smile and a shake of her head.* MARK *at once becomes clay in that hand.)*

MARK. *(Wonderingly)* So *that's* why the rest of us have seen so little of you! *(*NANCY *looks away, self-consciously.)*

MUFF. A great relief to your pride, eh, Mark? *(He does not deign to answer—goes to* L. *of* H.*)*

NANCY. You'll help me help him, won't you, Mark? Your kindness will be such a charity. It will make a man of him—perhaps even a business man.

MUFF. *(To* MARK*)* Nancy's formula is so charmingly simple. "Treat a mouse like a lion—he'll grow a mane over night."

NANCY. I've got no formula whatsoever. I'm simply——

MUFF. Want to make it fifty, Nancy?

NANCY. Muff's apparently trying to be funny.

MARK. *(*L. *of* H. *to* MUFF*)* With her usual success.

ALAN'S VOICE. *(Off left)* Mark!

MARK. Yes.

ALAN. Where are those chairs?

MARK. Coming right away! *(Over* L. *of* H.*)* You can count on me, my dear.

NANCY. That means a great deal to me, Mark, in many, many ways.

MARK. You have only to command me, Nancy.

MUFF. Speak, Eustace—speak! *(*MARK *glares at her, then bows slightly to* NANCY *and murmurs.)*

MARK. Till later—— *(He goes off left with the chairs, looking daggers at* MUFF.*)*

NANCY. *(Rising)* Well, *you* were a great help, weren't you? *(Going to* R.C. MUFF *laughs.)*

MUFF. Make it fifty?

NANCY. Yes!

MUFF. Good!

NANCY. Only you keep out, hear?

MUFF. You don't think I'm mercenary enough to make it *harder* for you, darling? Oh, no.

NANCY. *(Ironically)* No, I suppose not! *(*MUFF *laughs,* NANCY *turns on her. Sits chair down* R.C.*)* Never mind—when the crash comes, you'll go under with the rest of them.

MUFF. When's it due? I seem to remember some talk about "one week"——

NANCY. 'Till six-thirty tonight!

MUFF. —About six hours—you'll have to rustle for that fifty.

NANCY. I intend to! *(*ALAN *comes in left, from the garden coatless, and mopping his brow.)*

ALAN. Hello!

MUFF. *Happy* Fourth of July! *(*NANCY *rises.)*

ALAN. Hot Fourth of July, anyway. *(He calls off left. At railing on* L.*)* Tell him to straighten that ninth row. *(Gestures—measuring the distance off* L.*)*

NANCY. *(To* R. *of stool)* Muff—go find Richard, will you?

MUFF. *(Rising—to* L. *of* H.*)* Sure you don't need me here? *(*NANCY *points to the French window* U.L. MUFF *goes up to* W.*)*

MARK'S VOICE. *(Off left)* That all right?

ALAN. *(At railing* L.*)* Fine! Then your mother wants a man at the tent. Some of the stakes need tightening. Richard around?

MARK'S VOICE. Never mind. I'll be glad to go myself. *(*MUFF *looks at* NANCY*—knowingly. Smiles.* ALAN *turns wonderingly.)*

ALAN. *(To chair at* L. *of* T.*)* Well, what's come over him?

MUFF. *(To above chair above* T.*)* . Alan, doesn't this heavenly day just make you want to be kind to everyone? *(Looking at* NANCY.*)*

ALAN. It does not. *(He takes his coat from the chair at* L. *of* T. *and puts it on, crossing to* L.C.*)* You look rather worried, Nancy.

NANCY. *(Front of* R. *of* H.*)* I'm beginning to see that a man's greatest victory may be over his own family.

ALAN. Yes—and *I* advise you to call it quits.

*(*NANCY *smiles confidently. Sits* S. T. AUGUSTA *comes in from the garden* L., *wearing a sun hat and a pair of old gloves.* MARK *follows her.* ALAN *crosses above hammock to* R.C.3. KATIE *enters from door up* R., *crosses on porch.)*

AUGUSTA. We've all worked ourselves lame.

Where's that wretched infant? *(To* MUFF*)* Couldn't you find him?

*(*OLIVER *enters from the house with a small package of American flags.)*

MUFF. He isn't up yet.

AUGUSTA. What! *(*OLIVER *gives* MUFF *the package of flags.*

OLIVER. Take these out to Mother, Muff—— *(*OLIVER *looks back into the living-room. Calling.)* Oh, Katie! 'Here a minute! *(*KATIE *appears in the window up* L.*, carrying a breakfast tray in some disorder.)* What have you got there?

KATIE. *(To below* R. *of* W.—U.L.*)* Mr. Richard's breakfast tray.

OLIVER. *(*L. *of* KATIE. *Incredulously)* His breakfast *tray*——?

MARK. *(Above* L. *of* H.*, a glance at* NANCY *first.* NANCY *smiles encouragingly)* Poor kid, probably all tired out. *(Glances at* NANCY. OLIVER *looks at him amazed. A step down.)*

OLIVER. *(*L. *of chair above* T. *to* AUGUSTA*)* Hasn't he been helping you and Mother?

AUGUSTA. He *has* not.

MARK. Well, we managed all right without him. *(A glance at* NANCY.*)*

MUFF. *(At speaker's table* L.*)* Mark's one regret is not to have been there to butter his little toast for him. *(Looks from* MARK *to* NANCY. *She goes out into garden* L.*)*

OLIVER. He had his breakfast in *bed?*

KATIE. *(Front of* R. *of window* U.IL.*)* By the window—in your blue silk wrapper, Mr. Mark——

*(*MARK *starts angrily, catches* NANCY'S *eye, covers himself, smiling broadly.* KATIE *goes out window* U.L. *Exits to* L. OLIVER'S *mouth sets.)*

AUGUSTA. I don't know *what's* got into him. *(She goes into the house—window up* L.*)*

MARK. *(Above* L. *of* H.*)* Oh, let him alone, Augusta. He's welcome to that old rag if he wants it. *(*AUGUSTA *exits window* U.L. *He glances at* NANCY, *who smiles her thanks, then he calls after* AUGUSTA. *Goes up to the window* L.*)* Augusta—! Augusta! Let him alone! *(*OLIVER, L. *of* T., *crosses to* L.C.2, *glances at* NANCY *and then nods his head decisively, and crossing above* H., *goes out the window* B.R. MARK *following.)* Wait a minute, Noll. There's no sense in riding the kid *all* the time. *(A quick glance at* NANCY *over his shoulder.* NANCY *smiles. He exits up* U. *right.)* Noll—Noll!

NANCY. *(To* L. *of* H.*)* Well—the time has come.

ALAN. *(To* R. *of stool)* Now, you wait a minute, Nancy. If——

NANCY. The time has *come. (He looks at her, finds no quarter, and shrugs helplessly.)*

ALAN. If he discovers that you're manoeuvering him, too, when you're the first person in whom he's ever had the slightest confidence——

NANCY. I know. He won't discover it. Alan, you must tell him the moment he comes down. Naturally, he won't take all they've got and *keep* it—But he *may* threaten to—that's all *I* want!

ALAN. Remember that if he should—and get trounced, it'd be the last straw, the very last.

NANCY. But he might *win* a *real* fight! It's the little ones that are so easy to lose. *(She goes up* L.C., *crosses above* H. *to* U.R. *of* H.*)* I'll go up now. They won't dare make a scene if I'm there. Breakfast in bed—heavens! What commandment does that break?

(She goes out window B.R. *After a thoughtful moment, Alan goes up and takes two law books*

from arm chair up R.C. *There is a thump as of someone jumping to the ground off* R. RICHARD *enters garden* R.*)*

ALAN. *(At armchair up* R.C.*)* Well, where did *you* come from?

RICHARD. *(Crossing below* H. *to* L.C.*)* —Off the roof. Good jump. You must try it sometime, gives you confidence in your diving. *(Goes up* L.C., *looks off into garden.)*

ALAN. *(To above* C. *of* H.*)* Richard, I've concluded that in this household, you and I represent the down-trodden minority.

RICHARD. *(Crossing above hammock to* R.*)* 'Guess we do, all right.

ALAN. And our oppressors' main strength is money, isn't it? (RICHARD *goes up to* W.R.)

RICHARD. 'Spose it is. A fortune in pins! *(Shortly)* —Wish the man who invented 'em hadn't ever lost that button.

ALAN. I think there's a way to knock the pins from under them.

RICHARD. *(Dully)* Is there?

ALAN. The encounter would be very brief—and practically bloodless.

RICHARD. *(At* R. *of* H.*)* I wouldn't object to a little blood. *(*RICHARD *crosses and sits* L. *side of* H., *a brief pause.)*

ALAN. *(Looking about him)* Nice house of yours, this. *(No response from* RICHARD.*)* Lucky you weren't born a couple of years earlier.

RICHARD. Where's Nan—er—er my pup, Portly, d'you know?

ALAN. Lucky your father's lawyer chose the right time to die. Lucky the State protects a child born after a will is made.

RICHARD. What the devil you talking about?

ALAN. Do you remember the date of your birth?

RICHARD. No,—'twasn't important. *(*ALAN *takes the will from his pocket and indicates the date on it.)*

ALAN. Look at the date here——

RICHARD. What's this, Father's will?

ALAN. Ah ha.

RICHARD. Well, what about it? *(Looks at it.)*

ALAN. *(Gives him an open law book)* Here's the statute.

RICHARD. The what?

ALAN. The statute.

RICHARD. The statute of whom? (RICHARD *frowns over it, then looks at* ALAN *with wide, unbelieving eyes.* ALAN *gives him the other lawbook.)*

ALAN —A few of the cases with the decisions. See? Every one for the child.

RICHARD. What child? Well, what's the joke? *(A brief pause.)*

ALAN. *(Still above* C. *of* H.*)* You poor kid—does there always have to be a joke somewhere?

RICHARD. —Generally is, where I'm concerned, isn't there?

ALAN. Well, for once it's on someone else. *(*RICHARD *looks at him searchingly.)*

RICHARD. *(Is sitting* L. *of* H.*)* But—but—*Alan* —this is ridiculous! *(Closes book, throws it on hammock.)*

ALAN. 'Think so?

RICHARD. Else why didn't they discover it then?

ALAN. Because the will was so simple, I presume.

RICHARD. —And maybe I was too small to be noticed.

ALAN. Exactly. But they'll have trouble overlooking you *now.*

RICHARD. *(Hands him the book)* Find me that statute again. (ALAN *does so. Looking at book)* I'm—I'm—it's sort of confusing, isn't it?

ALAN. *(Above* R. *side of* H.*)* Your father died——

RICHARD. I know! I know!

ALAN. —Leaving a wife, five children, and about six hundred thousand——

RICHARD. 'Much as that? *(*ALAN *nods.)*

ALAN. —With the widow's third out, your share would be one-fifth of the remaining two-thirds——

RICHARD. What do I do, multiply or divide?

ALAN. *(Smiling)* In this case, you add—— *(Counting on his fingers.)* Plus interest for twenty-two years, plus your factory profits, plus the fact that the estate was diminished more than a third by losses in nineteen-seven and eight—— *(*RICHARD *looks about him fearfully. Puts hand on* ALAN'S, *stopping him.)*

RICHARD. Sh-h-h! Don't plus so loud.

ALAN. *(Is above hammock)* Richard, you could clean them out right down to the last cent. And there'd be thousands still due you.

RICHARD. They owe me money?

ALAN. Ah-ha.

RICHARD. Ha!

ALAN. As I remarked before, it's a nice house. The only fee I ask as your lawyer, is to be moved promptly out of it.

RICHARD. I don't blame you. But listen—if all this is true—you know—how much am I worth?

ALAN. Approximately—four hundred thousand.

RICHARD. My God!— But listen: Father *left* everything to Mother.

ALAN. Of course. But by this technicality——

RICHARD. Oh, I couldn't do that—— *(Closes book, lays it on* C. *of* H.*)* You *can't* do a thing like that to your own family——

ALAN. You *can,* well enough. The question is——

RICHARD. There's no question about it, Alan, you ought to be ashamed——

ALAN. Well, upon my word——

RICHARD. You really ought—— *(Again he looks fearfully about him.)* Besides, they'd raise the roof. Now look—you get this settled just as quietly as you can—give me something or other to sign—they needn't know about it till afterwards—I don't want to get them all riled up again—because—because I'm hoping they'll give me back my full allowance, see? *(A door closes inside off* R.*)*

ALAN. Do you *realize* what a chance you're losing?

RICHARD. Sh-h-h! —Look out! Here they come—— *(Rising,* ALAN *picks up the lawbooks, and will, puts will in pocket.)* Remember—*quietly!* Don't let 'em get on to it.—They'll blame it on me, and I can't help when I was born.

(He rapidly goes off left into the garden. ALAN *looks after him, shaking his head, goes to* R. *of* T.L.C., *has the lawbooks in his hands.* NANCY *enters from house, window* B.R.*)*

NANCY. *(To* R. *of* S.T.*)* Well?

ALAN. *(*L. *of front of* H.*)* —Just as I told you. He won't even consider it.

NANCY. Is he afraid to?

ALAN. It's partly that, I suppose. *(To* L. *of stool* C. *He laughs pityingly.)* He doesn't want to endanger his poor little allowance.

NANCY. *(Crossing to* R. *of chair* R. *of* T.*)* Don't —I could cry for him. Oh, that *devilish* family—I'll *make* him down them! I'll make *them* goad him him into it.

ALAN. *(Crosses to her)* The one way to get them to do a thing, is to advise them very firmly not to. *(*NANCY *goes* L. *thoughtfully.)* That's *my* method.

NANCY. All right, use it. I'll use my own. What allowance does he get?

ALAN. Used to be eighty a month. Forty, now.

NANCY. When's it due?

ALAN. Why—uh—tomorrow, I think.

NANCY. And what's the most precious thing in the world to him? His stories? (OLIVER *starts from* R. *at back.)*

ALAN. I suppose they are—why?

NANCY. *(Reflectively)* First—let's see what costs forty dollars that a well-brought-up girl can accept? *(Sits chair at* L. *of* T.L.C. OLIVER *enters from the window* B.L., *looking very much annoyed. He does not notice* ALAN *and* NANCY. *He comes down stage and places a chair with a bang, above table* L.C.*)* Ouch! (ALAN *goes up* L. *of* H. *Exits* W. *up* L.*)*

OLIVER. It *is* annoying, you know.

NANCY. Couldn't you find him?

OLIVER. His door was locked and he wouldn't answer.

NANCY. Tsch—tsch.

OLIVER. It's not so much these constant petty annoyances as—uh—my responsibility for his future.

NANCY. Of course—— *(A brief pause.)* You know what? —I think you and Mark spoil him—with your kindness. *(He looks at her inquiringly.)*

OLIVER. Well—— *(With a shallow laugh)* He's the youngest, you know.

NANCY. All the more reason for discipline.

OLIVER. *(Sits—chair at* R. *of* T.L.C.*)* It's a problem!

NANCY. —Another case of too much money and too much leisure, isn't it?

OLIVER. Exactly.

NANCY. At his age oughtn't he to be thinking of going into business?

OLIVER. When I was his age I'd been at work four years.

NANCY. It's this crazy writing-bee, in his bonnet.

OLIVER. That's just it! *(A brief pause.)*

NANCY. Do you know what *I'd* do with him?

OLIVER. What?

NANCY. —For his own good, of course.

OLIVER. Yes, certainly——

NANCY. *(Firmly)* First I'd stop his allowance—absolutely! Then if he was still troublesome, I'd tell him that I'd locked up all his books and manuscripts until he'd shown me he could earn his living like a man.

OLIVER. It's what he deserves. 'Might work, as a last resort.

NANCY. I wouldn't suggest it, if it weren't for knowing what a trial it must be for you all—to see one of you who doesn't—you know—measure up——

(MARK *enters by French window* B.R.)

OLIVER. I'm glad you understand. *(To* MARK, *not pleased at being interrupted.)* Well?

MARK. *(Below* S.T.*)* If he wants to stay in there, why not let him?

OLIVER. *(Rises)* Didn't I tell you to——

(OLIVER *stops and looks at* NANCY, *who tightens her fist, for his benefit.* OLIVER *nods his head to her, looks at* MARK, *then goes up* L.C., *crosses and goes out into the house window* B.R. MARK *turns, goes up toward the window, turns to* NANCY *with a helpless gesture.)*

NANCY. *(Crossing to* F. *of* R. *of* H.*)* I *can't* account for Oliver's attitude.

MARK. *(*R. *of* H. *After a moment)* Well—he's not going to bully the kid while I'm around, I can tell you that! *(He follows* OLIVER *into the house, calling)* Noll! *(A quick glance at* NANCY.*)* Noll!

(NANCY *looks after him for a moment, then turns smiling with satisfaction, murmuring "Forty dollars—forty dollars." After a moment* RICHARD *enters cautiously from the garden on* L., *gaining heart when he finds that* NANCY *is alone.*)

NANCY. (*Sits* R. *side of hammock*) Well, I thought you'd never appear.

RICHARD. What time is it?

NANCY. Nearly twelve.

RICHARD. Wicked. (*He has his pipe.*) —'Been talking business with Alan—he's my lawyer, you know. (*Sits beside her on hammock.* RICHARD *blows a great gust of smoke toward the ceiling.*) Awful bore on a holiday.

NANCY. It's a dog's life—this having responsibilities.

RICHARD. —I'm opposed to making even dogs do things they don't want to. When I try to get Eustace to beg on his hind legs and he won't, I give him the bone just the same. If I didn't, he'd have every right to my leg instead, wouldn't he?

NANCY. My dear, he'd faint at the very thought of it.

RICHARD. (*Is sitting* L. *side of* H.) I said "a right to." —Then take my pup, Portly. Maybe I want him to play ball with me. But he spends a whole gorgeous day out in the meadow, stalking a beetle.

NANCY. (*Is sitting* R. *side of* H.) —As the good Lord intended he should.

RICHARD. —As *he* intended he should. No interference. If he wants to go beetling, let him beetle. I appreciate the fact that our points of view differ.

NANCY. You're unusual, Richard—you really are.

RICHARD. Nope, just proper respect individual

preference: hind legs, all fours—a ball or a beetle—let the dog decide.

NANCY. I'm very fond of Portly. I wonder if you could find another like him——

RICHARD. I'll get you his brother!

NANCY. Do they come very high?

RICHARD. I got Portly for three dollars.

NANCY. *(Disappointed)* Oh—I thought he was —fifty at least. . . .

RICHARD. I can get his brother for two and his sister's only one—I'll give you both.

NANCY. No—no. —On second thought, they probably wouldn't be like him at all. Thanks just the same. *(A pause. Finally* RICHARD *speaks bravely and deliberately.)*

RICHARD. —Nancy—I'll give you Portly himself. . . .

NANCY. *(Genuinely touched)* Oh, you *are* sweet. . . .

RICHARD. *(Looking away)* He's a *nice* little dog——

NANCY. I wouldn't think of taking him——

RICHARD. But I'd *like* you——

NANCY. I wouldn't think of it!

RICHARD. *(Much relieved)* Well—if you won't, you won't—Like a balloon instead? *(He detaches a balloon sticking in pocket on* R. *side of hammock at back, and gives it to her.)* —Great day here, you know. *(Rises, goes to* R. *of* T.L.C.*)* Balloons for the children, lemonade for the working-men——

NANCY. —Pleasure for all.—Why do they come here for it?

RICHARD. "Of all places"—you mean?

NANCY. You know what I mean—the Celebration.

RICHARD. Great-Grandfather-Winslow, born 1811, died 1878. Height, 6 feet 2. Complexion, ruddy. Wives, three. Public offices, many—Mayor, the first.

NANCY. He must have been a great buck in his day.

RICHARD. *(To* L. *of* H. *Affecting* OLIVER'S *stiff voice)* Jabez Winslow was a very notable figure in the City's early development. *(He laughs, and continues in his own tone. Sits on* L. *arm of* H.*)* —And made a notable figure out of it—the old grafter. Fourth of July's a kind of annual coronation for the Royal House of Jabez. (NANCY *laughs.)* —You mustn't laugh, though—*I* did once—— *(He pauses, reminiscently.)* You've probably noticed how hard they take their prominence. 'N when the bourgeoisie march up here from town to look upon the Lord's Annointed, it's a ver-ry serious affair. *(*NANCY *looks toward the table against the railing on* L.*)*

NANCY. —And of course Oliver makes a speech——

RICHARD. Reads it! Here—— *(He takes the long scroll from the case on the table* L.C., *unfurls it and indicates the old wooden-ends to* L. *of* H.*)* —These end-pieces b'longed to Jabez himself. Good excuse for Noll—when he faces a crowd his mind goes completely blank. But you've no idea how important the occasion is to him. 'Nother Gettysburg. For weeks afterward he can't pass a child on the street without stopping 'n putting his hand on his head 'n smiling kindly down at him. *(He scans the scroll.)* "Friends, we welcome you. On this auspicious occasion—" —They always begin, "On this auspicious occasion." *(He reads further)* "Industrial progress—Municipal Welfare"—factories—business, more factories, more business, bigger factories, bigger business, business, business, business—Agh! *(In revulsion, he tosses the speech upon the swing, crosses above to* L. *of* T.*)* 'S if there wasn't too much business already . . . Smoke 'n steam 'n scurry 'n scamper——

NANCY. *(Rises, to* R. *of* T.L.C.*)* What the world needs, is less effort, and more fun. *(Strikes balloon on table.)*

RICHARD. *(Is leaning against* L. *column)* —More leisure, fewer alarm clocks.

NANCY. Less do-as-you're told, more do-as-you-please.

RICHARD. *(Is leaning against column* L.*)* —The way *we* do.

NANCY. Yes—the way we do. *(She looks at him tenderly, a little pityingly, perhaps.)* Oh, you dear boy you. *(For a long instant* RICHARD *looks into her eyes. When he finally speaks, it is with difficulty.)*

RICHARD. *(To* L.L. *of* T.*)* You've—been awfully nice to me——

NANCY. Isn't everyone?

RICHARD. But I think you're one of the few people in the world who's nice without any reason but—just being nice. No—what—you—call—it—ulterior motive. Nothing but just dear, understanding niceness.

NANCY. Oh, I can be nasty, too! But you see I do like you so much . . . *(A pause. He is unable to reply.)* You can believe that.

RICHARD. I do believe it. And Nancy, I—well—I——*(*NANCY *decides to tread on safer ground. He draws chair up to* R. *of table. Sits.)*

NANCY. *(Sticks the balloon in pitcher)* I read the new story last night before bed. Isn't "Ride a Cock-Horse" the newest one?

RICHARD. Yes. Did you like it?

NANCY. I don't know when I've had a better time. I wept buckets.

RICHARD. Mean it——?

NANCY. Honestly! *(Extends her hand.)* When

I lie, my hand trembles. Does it? (RICHARD *gingerly examines it—afraid to touch it. She makes a gesture to say, "Well, then?")*

RICHARD. Wonder'll anyone take that story——

NANCY. What does that matter, if *you* know it's good?

RICHARD. *(Dubiously)* Um. Somebody's got to take something soon. *(Sits, chair* L. *of* T.L.C. NANCY *glances at him sideways, then speaks with studied unconcern.)*

NANCY. Publish it yourself—for your friends. —I've been told that for forty or fifty dollars——

RICHARD. 'Hate that sort of thing. If the world doesn't want it in the usual way—let the world go without.

NANCY. "Ride a Cock-Horse"—— I love Mother Goose, don't you? *(He nods enthusiastically)* —There was the most heavenly edition at Scribner's just before I came away.

RICHARD. *(Eagerly)* What was it like?

NANCY. *(Gestures)* About so big—huge print, illustrated with real woodcuts.

RICHARD. Sounds gorgeous! Why didn't you buy it?

NANCY. Too expensive.

RICHARD. Couldn't be! I'll get it for you! (NANCY *glances at him quickly.)*

NANCY. Promise?

RICHARD. Yes.

NANCY. Really?

RICHARD. Yes.

NANCY. You *will?*

RICHARD. Yes.

NANCY. It's an outrageous price.

RICHARD. What's outrageous?

NANCY. Forty-two dollars. *(A brief pause)* —I *said* it was expensive.

RICHARD. I'll send for it tomorrow. My—my

income's due then. *(A sigh of relief from* NANCY.*)*

NANCY. Thanks for it—I'll love it better than anything I have. . . . I suppose Mark and Oliver would call that arrested development. . . .

RICHARD. Pooh! What do they know?

NANCY. Aren't the—conflicting tastes awkward, sometimes? *(A worried, reminiscent look comes into* RICHARD'S *eyes.)*

RICHARD. *(Rising—crossing to* S.T.*)* Sometimes —a little! (NANCY *watches him intently. He is counting his resources mentally. He sits* S.T.*)*

NANCY. You know, *I* think a man's greatest victory is over *his own family.*

RICHARD. *(Lowly)* Maybe it is.

NANCY. *(Rising, crossing to* L. *of* DICK) I suppose you've always simply overridden yours—— (RICHARD *laughs shortly and shrugs—sits* S.T.*)* I wouldn't be ashamed of it. I think to be great you have to be remorseless.

RICHARD. *(Rising—to* R. *of* S.T.*—dubiously)* Do you really think so?

NANCY. Every great man seems to be. When he knows he's right and people oppose him, what does he do?—Just simply extinguishes them——

RICHARD. "Extinguishes 'em" . . .

NANCY. Don't you hate people without that—audacity?

RICHARD. (R. *of* S.T.) —Awful.

NANCY. *(Front of* R. *of* H.) *Ends* are the important things—if *they're* right the means never matter. I don't hold with this "Destiny which shapes our ends"—— *I* say, shape Destiny!

RICHARD. *(Nodding gravely)* That's right. That's my rule of life. *(A pause. He says softly)* "Extinguishes 'em"—puts 'em out. *(A door closes inside. He glances nervously towards the house.)* There's—there comes Mark—— *(He puts a stern countenance which gradually changes to one of ap-*

prehension.) I—I don't care to see him just now— *(He crosses front toward French window,* B.L. MARK *enters* W.B.R.)

MARK. *(Crossing above* H. *to* RICHARD*—genially rubbing his hands)* Hello, Old Son—— Had a great sleep, didn't you? (RICHARD *is struck in his tracks by this unexpected greeting. He turns.)*

RICHARD. *(Scowling)* What's it to you?

MARK. It's the right idea. *(Offers him cigarette case.)*

RICHARD. What do *you* know 'bout "right ideas," you poor pinhead? *(He turns and regards the dumfounded* MARK *sadly.)* —We've had the pin factory for years—and I'm only just thinking of "pinheads" . . . *(Grins at* NANCY. *Goes into house* U.B.L.)

MARK. *(To front of* L. *of* H.) You see the thanks you get.

NANCY. *(Sits* R. *side of* H.) You mustn't mind if at first he's a little suspicious of kindness. Oliver is so *strict* with him.

MARK. Quite a disciplinarian, Noll.

NANCY. I suppose the next thing he'll do will be to stop his allowance.

MARK. *(Knowingly)* He may, you know—may do it this very morning.

NANCY. And a good thing perhaps—everything considered. The only difficulty is that Richard'll think he's just being—malicious.

MARK. I'll tell him we're not. I'll explain that we are acting out of kindness.

NANCY. Somehow, I'm afraid that won't convince him. *(A thoughtful pause. She rises, goes to him—pats his arm.)* Listen, Mark! If there's a scene, you just be as decent as you can, all through it. Then, after the big blow comes, say: Remember, Richard, "A man's greatest victory is over his own selfishness." *(Takes out his handkerchief, folds it, then replaces it in his breast pocket.)*

MARK. "A man's greatest victory over his own selfishness" . . . not bad—not at all bad.

NANCY. You won't forget? —I should hate to have you and Oliver appear in a bad light.

MARK. I'll tell him, all right.

NANCY. *(Looks off left)* Oh—your Mother! And I haven't lifted a finger with the decorations! You haven't seen me.—Remember!

(NANCY *goes into the house* W.B.R. *For a moment* MARK *is left alone, murmuring to himself. Crosses above* H. *to* R.C.*)*

MARK. "A man's greatest victory is over his own selfishness."

(MRS. WINSLOW *enters from the garden on* L., *goes down* L. *of* T.L.C. AUGUSTA *enters window* L., *is carrying a tray with pitcher of ice water and four glasses, also two silk American flags. She places the tray on the speaker's table at* L. ALAN *enters window* U.L., *following* AUGUSTA. OLIVER *enters from window up* R. *to above* H.*)*

MRS. WINSLOW. There! We're ready for them now. *(Taking newspaper from table* L.C., *crossing to* S.T. *at* R. *of* H.*)*

AUGUSTA. —And nearly time, too. *(She shudders.)* —If only they wouldn't have a *brass* band.

ALAN. *(Above* L. *of hammock)* Well, Noll, I hope you'll have a pleasant word for Washington, Lincoln and God.

(OLIVER *crosses to above the table* L.C., *looks for his speech in the vase and is alarmed to find it missing. He finally discovers it upon the swing, picks it up and returns to the table with it.* ALAN *takes a cigarette from smoking table, lights it.)*

MRS. WINSLOW. *(She takes the ashtray from* S.T. *at* R. *of hammock and during her speech goes to the railing on* R.*, empties it and returns it to its place on* S.T. AUGUSTA *sits—chair at* L. *of table* L. C. *and unrolls the American flags)* —But I don't know what we're all coming to—we, who are an example to the townspeople!—Suppose the working-man knew that my youngest son lay asleep until nearly twelve, and had his breakfast in bed, like a Prince of Darkness? It's things like that, that cause strikes. *(Sits* R. *side of* H.*)*

OLIVER. When Richard finds his allowance is stopped, he may be less luxurious. *(Hands* AUGUSTA *the balloon in pitcher.)*

ALAN. *(Is above* H.*)* Really—I can't advise you too strongly, not to coerce Richard any further.

MRS. WINSLOW. Steps *must* be taken.

MARK. *(Crossing front to* R. *of* T.L.C.*)* I happen to know that all that's needed to get him to work, is just one more little push.

ALAN. I must warn against pushing.

AUGUSTA. "Warn"? *(Rises, sticks balloon stick in the foliage on hedge at* L.*, then puts the flags in the holders on hedge* L.*)*

ALAN. My advice is to treat him with the same deference you'd pay a steel trap.

MARK. Woof, woof. *(To above* L. *of* H.*)*

ALAN. There—that's all I can say. *(Goes to* U.R. *of* H.*)*

MARK. The oracle has spoken.

OLIVER. —And rubbish, as usual.

*(*RICHARD *enters window up* R. *A very cocky* RICHARD. *He comes down* R. *of* H. MUFF *enters,*

garden on L. *to* R. *of* OLIVER. AUGUSTA *sits—chair at* L. *of* T.L.C.)

RICHARD. *(Crossing front to* L.C.) It must be ninety in the shade. I'm for a swim. *(*OLIVER *looks up from his writing.* ALAN *sits on* S.T. *at* R. *of* H.)

OLIVER. The pool's closed today.

RICHARD. Closed, your Grandmother. *(He continues on his way to* L. *of* H.)

OLIVER. The pool is *closed*.

MRS. WINSLOW. Richard! *(He turns.)* Did you *hear* what Oliver said? *(*MUFF *crosses above hammock to* L. *of* MARK.)

RICHARD. *(At* L. *of* H.) Mother, what possible harm can there be in . . .

MRS. WINSLOW. We won't have this old discussion again, if you please.

(RICHARD *opens his mouth to protest, but closes it again, instead, and moves cautiously toward* OLIVER. KATIE *enters from the house, window up* L.)

KATIE. There's a 'phone call from Amity, Ma'am.

(MRS. WINSLOW *rises, going up* L.C., *murmurs to herself. "'Amity'—it must be Aunt Emma." Pats* OLIVER'S *arm as she passes.* OLIVER *and* MARK *ad lib. "give her my love."* AUGUSTA *ad lib—Aunt Emma again.* MUFF *to* R. *of* ALLAN *ruffles his hair, singing, "Aunt Emma is coming. Hurray, hurray!"* MRS. WINSLOW *exits window up* L. KATIE *follows* MRS. WINSLOW *out.* MUFF *sits* R. *side of hammock.)*

OLIVER. *(Reading his speech, mumbles to himself)* Friends, we welcome you. . . .

RICHARD. Say, Noll—— (OLIVER *ignores him—continues mumbling.)* Noll!

OLIVER. *(Looking up)* Eh, what?

RICHARD. I'd like my full month's allowance tomorrow, 'stead of week by week. You know, the whole thing, all at once. (OLIVER *turns heavily about and contemplates him.)*

OLIVER. You would, would you? *(Continues mumbling.)*

ALAN. That's a perfectly reasonable request.

(OLIVER *finishes the sentence he is reading, then turns to* RICHARD.)

OLIVER. Why do you want it?

RICHARD. I want it for—for—what difference does that make?

MARK. *(Is above* L. *of* H. *Kindly)* He's entitled to a reason, old fellow.

RICHARD. (L. *of* H.) Well—I want to buy a book, old fellow.

MUFF. *(Is sitting* R. *side of* H. *to* OLIVER) Another! Wanton waste, isn't it?

OLIVER. *(Studying his speech)* Why should you need so much for one book?

RICHARD. *(Eagerly)* It's not a usual one. It's a special Mother Goose.

AUGUSTA. *(Is sitting chair* L. *of* T.L.C.) *Mother Goose!*

MARK. *(Above* L. *of* H.) You won't get anywhere by joking, Richard.

ALAN. —You don't mean the *regular* Mother Goose?

RICHARD. Yes, I do. (ALAN *sinks back.)*

AUGUSTA. Wouldn't you rather have a nice little red Kiddie-Kar?

OLIVER. This is about the limit. *(To* RICHARD) Now get this into your head: you *can't* have the whole month's allowance. In fact, you can't have any. . . .

RICHARD. *(To* R. *of* OLIVER*)* What!

OLIVER. It has automatically stopped—until you give some indication of being old enough, and sane enough, to expend it properly.

MARK. *(*U.L. *of* H.*)* We ask very little; if you'll simply come into the factory——

RICHARD. *(Furious)* Oh, you—— *(He controls himself. Voice lower.)* 'Mother know this?

OLIVER. It's her money. I never do anything without her advice and consent.

MUFF. Ha, ha. *(*MARK *looks at her.)* Sorry. It slipped.

RICHARD. Are you sure it *is* Mother's money?

AUGUSTA. Cryptic, isn't he?

RICHARD. I may be more clear in a minute! In fact, in fact, I—— *(He hesitates, his courage dwindling before* OLIVER'S *impassive countenance.)*

OLIVER. You heard Mark's offer. Take it—or leave it. *(*RICHARD *bows his head.)*

RICHARD. *(*L. *of* H.*)* I've got to get that book.

MARK. *(Above* C. *of* H.*)* When you've been at the office a week, I'll be glad to lend you something till pay day.

RICHARD. *(Rallying)* Oh, *will* you? Who're you—to lend *me* money? *(To* OLIVER*)* Listen: I'll put up with this 'n do nothing, if you'll pay me my month's allowance, 'n promise me a room here for my own—a permanent room, big enough to turn 'round in.

OLIVER. I see no reason to make any promises whatsoever.

MARK. Besides, you know Aunt Emma——

*(*MRS. WINSLOW *re-enters from window up* L.*)*

RICHARD. Then it's your own fault if I have to do it! *(Crossing to* R.C.L.*)*

OLIVER. Do what?

(WARN Band.)

ALAN. *(Rising)* Noll—if you know what's good for you——

OLIVER. When I need suggestions, I'll ask for them. (ALAN *goes up* R., *crosses above* H. *to* L.C.4.)

MRS. WINSLOW. *(Coming down* L.C.*)* Did someone say "Aunt Emma"? *(To* R. *of* OLIVER*)*—That was Emma, now. She's coming next Monday, after all. *(Going to front of* L. *of* H.*)* Richard—you'll have to give Alan the little room at the head of the stairs and go to the Spencers' for a few days. *(Sits* L. *side of* H. ALAN *crosses above to speaker's table on* L.*)*

RICHARD. *(Crosses and sits stool* C., *facing her. Gently)* Mother, they've stopped my allowance. Don't you think that's enough—'thout putting me out of the house altogether?

MRS. WINSLOW. *(Uncertainly)* Why—if one of the others will go——

RICHARD. I ask one of you—please—to do it. Just once, in my place. *(Rising, goes to* L. *of* H.*)* Just once—to show me that you *could*—— *(To* MRS. WINSLOW.*)* See? *(*RICHARD *turns hopelessly and sits on the left arm of hammock.)* Listen, Mother—I'm about at the end of my rope. 'Tisn't your fault, I know—but if I can't have anything of my own here—won't you give me an allowance—just a small one—so small you won't even miss it—and let me go away somewhere?

MRS. WINSLOW. *(Patting his hand)* But darling—I don't want you to leave us——

RICHARD. Nor do I want to—but will you do it, Mother?

MRS. WINSLOW. I don't see why you can't get along with your brothers. And I'm sure you shouldn't go off by *yourself*.

RICHARD. I wouldn't go far—and I'd come home

often—I'd see you often, really I would. I just want—a room—to myself—somewhere.

ALAN. *(Is sitting on speaker's table)* That seems little enough to ask.

OLIVER. *(First gestures* ALAN *to be quiet)* Living alone would be the worst thing in the world for him.

RICHARD. This is between Mother 'n me. You keep your stupid nose out.

MRS. WINSLOW. Hush, Richard—you mustn't speak so of Oliver's nose.—If Oliver thinks——

RICHARD. It's what *you* think—it's you I'm asking. *Will* you? (MRS. WINSLOW *glances furtively at* OLIVER. *He, the picture of Reliability and Good Judgement, slowly shakes his head.)*

MRS. WINSLOW. Why, my dear, I think we'd better leave it to Oliver. He knows what's best for you. *(*RICHARD *with bowed head goes up* L.C. *and crosses above the hammock to up* R. *of it.* MARK, *crossing above* RICHARD, *pats him on the shoulder, goes to* U.L. *of* H.*)*

OLIVER. I have your own best interests at heart—bear that in mind.

MUFF. What *would* our interests do without you, Oliver?

AUGUSTA. Another pretty scene. A pity Nancy missed it. *(*RICHARD *stops like a shot and half turns.)*

MARK. *(At* L. *of* RICHARD, *hand on his shoulders—patronizingly—gently)* It's hard. I know, Richard—but remember—a man's greatest victory is over his own——

RICHARD. *(Interrupting)* "Over his own——"!

MARK. Yep! *(*RICHARD *crosses to* L. *of* H. MARK *crosses to upper* R. *of* H.*)*

RICHARD. *(Suddenly he turns upon the family)* Now you listen to me, my dear family, and don't you interrupt. Ever since I remember, you've taken unholy pleasure finding new ways to mortify me. *(From the distance, the faint strains of a brass band begin to be heard. The tune is Sousa's "Stars and Stripes Forever." In the ensuing scene, the family, with the exception of* MUFF *and* ALAN, *are more interested in the approach of the band than they are in* RICHARD. *Note: In addition to the brass band, about ten extras are needed. To cue the ensuing scene, there are five switches off stage, each connected to a different colored lamp in cellar. Signals for band—as far away as possible when band starts, the second switch up close for finish. Other three switches for the crowd. Amber for murmurs. Blue for cheers. White for laughs. The bass drum is* heard in the house, at first as softly as possible. *The brasses come in gradually.)* 'Cause I was the youngest. 'Cause I was different 'n' the rest of you. 'Cause you're naturally mean—and I didn't hit back. You've done every aggravating thing you could—to—to—standardize me—to make me "average"—like you are. Well, I'm above average, see? I've got a better mind than any of you—with possible exception of Augusta——

AUGUSTA. *(Ironically)* Oh—thanks . . . *(Rising—goes to railing on* L. *and looks off. To the family)* That's the band, all right. They're coming——

RICHARD. *(Crosses to* R.C.2*)* —And I mean to use it in my own way. I'm "the queer one"—you can't make me out, so you divert yourselves bullying me. Persecution, that's what it is! Don't know whether Mark's been the worst with his eternal petty nagging——

MARK. *(Above* L. *of* H.*)* Richard—you've got the wrong idea entirely . . . *(To above chair above* T.L.C., *watching off* L., RICHARD *waves the remark aside.)*

RICHARD. *(Goes to front of chair* R. *of* T.L.C.,

drags it around during his speech.—At the end of his speech he is almost in tears) —Or you, Oliver, with your blundering stupidity 'n your idea I'm a lump of mud it's your God-given duty to finger into shape. Maybe it's been Augusta, *(*AUGUSTA *sits—chair at* L. *of* T.L.C.*)* with her infernally sharp tongue. *(Kicks chair out of his way and goes to* L. *of* H.*)* Mother's done nothing but follow your orders. Muff's been decent as she could be, with her love for what's funny. But you've all had your methods—— *(He stops, bows his head, swallows hard and tries to control his trembling.)*

MARK. *(To* L. *of* DICK*)* We simply want to make a success of you. Do you object to that?

RICHARD. *(*L. *of* H.*)* Yes! That's just the point! Nobody's got any right to make anything of anyone! My future's *my* job. If I fail at it, all right. I'd rather fail in *my* own way than hit the sky in someone else's!

*(*MARK *turns up* L.C. RICHARD *sits—chair at* R. *of* T.L.C. MRS. WINSLOW *rises, goes to him, tries to quiet him. People among the crowd are heard greeting each other off left— "Hello, Tom! —See you at the office tomorrow, Jim!" etc.)*

AUGUSTA. There's philosophy for you. *(Murmurs from crowd.)*

MRS. WINSLOW. Poor child—his nerves are all upset. *(Going up* L. *of* H., *crosses above table to railing on* L. *Peering out.)* —They've turned into the drive. Mark—the awning—— *(*MARK *crosses, raises the awning and fastens it.)*

AUGUSTA. *(Rising, starts up* L.*)* I've got some bromides upstairs.

MUFF. *(Rising, to* L. *of* H.*)* I'll get one. . . .

RICHARD. *(Rises—crosses to* R.C.2*)* No! No!

'Not going to be stopped now. That's the way of it—whenever I assert myself, you treat me's though I'm sick. (MUFF *sits* C. *of* H.) Well—I'm through. *(To front of* S.T.) I don't look for understanding any more—don't expect any regard for different points of view—individual preference—*my right* to *do my own work in my own way.* Ask *simply* to be *let alone.* And you won't even promise me a room to myself—— *(A pause.)* Will you? *(*MUFF *and* ALAN *alone are listening to him.)*

MARK. *(Crossing to* L. *of stool* C.*)* —What? —Listen, old man, you aren't practical. With guests in the house——

RICHARD. *(Crossing, pushes* MARK *out of his way, goes to* R. *of* T.L.C. MARK *goes up* R. *of* H., *crossing above—watching off* L.*)* —Or enough money to go off somewhere on my own—money you can easily afford—as a loan, if you like. You won't let me have it—— *(A pause.) Will* you?

ALAN. *(To chair at* L. *of* T.L.C.*—Softly, to* OLIVER) Give it to him, Noll. Give it to him. *(*OLIVER *preserves a stony countenance, merely raising his brows a little over his speech. Turns to* MRS. WINSLOW.*)* Mother Winslow! —I tell you this is *serious. . . .*

(BAND.)

MRS. WINSLOW. I think, Alan, we understand Richard's needs as well as you do—— *(*ALAN *goes up* L.C. *Nervously)* I do hope that tent pole is firm. Augusta—you're sure the lemonade has enough sugar? *(*AUGUSTA *nods. Murmurs.* MRS. WINSLOW, *crossing above table, goes to* RICHARD. MARK *crosses above table to railing on* L. *Murmurs from the crowd.)* I am certain that when you and Oliver talk it over calmly——

RICHARD. *(Is at* L. *of* H.*)* I know what *that* means . . . Promise me one or the other now? *(The band grows louder.)*

AUGUSTA. Heavens, what music! (MRS. WINSLOW *crosses front of table to railing below* MARK. MUFF *crosses above table to railing on* L.)

MARK. Look at Mayor Duncan—big as life. (OLIVER *folds up the speech, so* RICHARD *can handle it and puts it in the pitcher.)*

MRS. WINSLOW. He's too old to march all this distance.

MUFF. And fat.

RICHARD. *(To front of* R. *of* H.) —All right, then, here goes!—I've got a little piece of news for you!

MARK. *(Simultaneously)* Lord! Half the factory's out. (OLIVER *rises to above his chair, bows to somebody in the crowd.)*

AUGUSTA. Oh! That infernal tune! And we wonder that Europe calls us vulgar—— *(Goes up* L.C.)

MUFF. *(Simultaneously)* There's Judge Ainslee! And look!—Mrs. Potts—with the banner——

MRS. WINSLOW. *(Simultaneously)* Do you remember last year? The salad? Oh, I *do* hope you chose a cool spot for it!

RICHARD. *(Is front of stool* C.) *Listen* to me! Listen, will you?

OLIVER. *(Above* R. *of his chair)* Don't let them see you till after my speech. *(Backing away to* R. *and* T. *The Family retreat from the railing. Murmurs from the crowd.)*

RICHARD. *(To* OLIVER) Listen, you!—*Will* you listen?

OLIVER. *(To* R. *of table)* Oh, do keep quiet for a *minute! (To front of table.)*

RICHARD. I'm not *going* to make pins! (NANCY *enters window up* R., *comes to above* C. *of* H., *watching* RICHARD.) I'm going to write—do you understand? And you can't stop me! I can stop you, though! You think you own this house, don't you? You think you own everything. Well, as it happens—*I'm* the one who—— *(He stops suddenly as he sees* NANCY, *goes to* R., *sits on bench.* MUFF *hastens to her and takes her arm. Murmurs from crowd.)*

MUFF. They're nearly here! Come on—let's get a front seat! *(Ad lib. all. She hurries the reluctant* NANCY *toward the garden steps on* L.*)*

OLIVER. *(To* R. *of* T. *Amiably)* I count on you two to start the applause! *(He begins to adjust his tie, and smooth down his hair. Band.)*

NANCY. *(At step on* L.*)* Oliver—isn't it time for—the last resort?

MUFF. *(Off* L.*)* Come on, Nancy.

NANCY. I'm coming.

(She goes out with MUFF. OLIVER *turns to* RICHARD.*)*

OLIVER. *(Crosses front of* H. *to* RICHARD, *who is sitting on bench* R.*)* You'll *write,* will you? Well, it happens that I've locked up every bit of writing and every book you own! You'll get them again when you've learned to talk sense. *(He crosses front of* H. *to above his chair, and watches the crowd approach. Murmurs from crowd—greetings, etc.)*

RICHARD. *(To front of* H.*)* You dared——! *(A pause. He is all but overcome with anger. He takes several deep breaths and swallows hard, then lowly)* Oliver—— (OLIVER *does not turn. Sees a friend in the crowd, waves his hand to him—Louder)* Oliver——! *(No answer. Sharply)* Oliver—! (OLIVER *turns impatiently.)* Will you give my things back to me? *(*OLIVER *turns away.)* This *instant?*

OLIVER. *(Over his shoulder)* No! (RICHARD *crosses to* R. *of* T.L.C., *seizes the speech and hides it behind his back. Backs away to* C.I. AUGUSTA *has turned to* OLIVER *in time to see* RICHARD *take the speech, but does not realize what it means.)*

RICHARD. Oliver—*Oliver! (Again* OLIVER *turns.) Will you give me them back?*

OLIVER. *(At* L. *of his chair)* You start at the office on Monday, or I'll burn the lot of them—think *that* over. *(He crosses to* L. *of* AUGUSTA, *the better to see.* AUGUSTA *goes above chair above table* L.C.*)*

RICHARD. *(In a fury.* C.I.*)* You——! *(Behind his back, he wrenches the wooden ends from the scroll and drops them upon the floor. Murmurs. He folds the speech together. The band is now nearer. Slowly, carefully,* RICHARD *tears the paper straight through. He brings his hands from behind his back, and tears it in two directions. Murmurs from the crowd.)*

(BAND.)

AUGUSTA. *(*L. *of chair above table* L.C.—L. *of* H. *Shrilly)* It's your speech!

OLIVER. What? *(Rushes at* RICHARD, *crossing above table.* RICHARD *runs up* R. *of* H. *to up* C. *of it.* MARK *rushes at* RICHARD. OLIVER *stops front of* H. AUGUSTA *has come down* L. *of table, crosses front to* L.C.S. MRS. WINSLOW *to* L.C.4. *All crowd around, exclaiming.)*

RICHARD. *(Still tearing. Simultaneous with the following three speeches)* Now, will you—*now* will you?

OLIVER. *(Front of* H.*)* I'll break your neck for you, that's what I'll do!

MRS. WINSLOW. *(*O.C.4. *Simultaneous with preceding speech by* DICK*)* Oliver! Oliver! Do you want them to hear you? Richard, how could you?

AUGUSTA. *(*L.C.3*)* Quick, Mark! We can piece it together. *(Above* C. *of* H. RICHARD *flings the pieces into the air, then runs laughingly to* R.C.2. MARK, ALAN, AUGUSTA *start frantically to pick them up.)*

RICHARD. *(At* R.C.2*) There's* your "Bigger Business"! There's your "Municipal Welfare"! There's your "Auspicious Occasion"!

AUGUSTA. He's gone mad!

ALAN. Looks like a total loss, to me. *(*AUGUSTA *and* MARK *pick up the pieces and try to piece the speech together, laying them on the table.)*

OLIVER. *(Advancing)* Well, young man——

MRS. WINSLOW. *(Crossing above* H.*, goes to* RICHARD*)* Richard! go to your room at once!

RICHARD. *(Is* R.C.2*—Sweetly)* But, you see, I haven't *got* any room. *(*MRS. WINSLOW *goes up* R.*)*

OLIVER. *(Is front of* H. *Advancing again)* I'll fix you so that——

AUGUSTA. *(To* OLIVER*)* Oliver! Don't be an idiot! You've got a speech to make! *(*OLIVER *turns, goes up* L.C.*, crosses above, comes down* L. *of table.* MRS. WINSLOW *goes up* R.*, slowly crosses above* L.*)*

MARK. *(To* RICHARD*)* We'll take care of you later. *(*RICHARD *merely smiles, and sits on* S.T. OLIVER *is staring into space, frowning, as he comes down* L. *of* T.*)*

AUGUSTA. *(Above table)* You remember it, don't you?

OLIVER. No!

RICHARD. *(Is sitting on* S.T.*)* Give 'em a brief account of Cap'n John Smith's early struggles with the Indians. *(*MARK *scowls.)* —Or tell 'em how pins are made, and why—— *(Murmurs.)*

MARK. *(Is* R. *of* T.IC.*, frantically trying to put the pieces together) You'd* better be saying your prayers. *(Murmurs from the crowd.)*

OLIVER. Wait a minute! *(Takes a piece of the speech* AUGUSTA *has placed at upper end of table. It is supposed to contain the first few words. He crosses front of table, takes the chair at* R. *of* T.*, draws it down and sits facing* L. *Slowly and heav-*

ily) "My friends—we welcome you—this auspicious occasion may introduce to a city," *(Band. He crumples the piece in his hand. He tries to remember)*—a city—a city—— *(*MARK *repeats after him, to encourage him.* MRS. WINSLOW *goes to him encouragingly)*—to a city ever richer—ever richer—ever richer—*(*MARK *and* AUGUSTA *repeat it)*—in—in public spirit of its citizens—new—new ideas for the municipal welfare.

RICHARD. *(Softly)* Hurray! *(*MRS. WINSLOW *turns imploring eyes upon him. He subsides.)*

OLIVER. And I am sure of—sure of—— *(All wait expectantly. A pause. The band has now nearly arrived, which serves only to increase* OLIVER'S *wretchedness.)*

ALAN. *(At* L. *of* T.*)* —Of what, Noll?

MRS. WINSLOW. *(Is at* R. *of* OLIVER*)* It's splendid, so far——

AUGUSTA. You'll remember it! Think—think! *(A pause.* OLIVER *stares into space, his face contorted with thought. The family watch him fearfully. The band has almost arrived and from now to the finish it grows louder, quite rapidly.)*

MRS. WINSLOW. Think! Think!

OLIVER. *(Finally)* It's gone from me entirely. *(*MARK *has several pieces of the speech that he has placed together.* AUGUSTA *reaches over and takes one of them to try it with hers.* MARK *grabs it away from her and returns it to its place.)*

RICHARD. *(Softly)* Now he belongs to the Ages.

OLIVER. *(Rising* L. *of chair)* Oh, *you'll* pay for this——

RICHARD. What are you asking, Noll? *(*OLIVER *goes to* L.I.*)*

AUGUSTA. *(To* OLIVER*)* It will come back. It *must!*

RICHARD. Pity Aunt Emma's not here with her ten-minute talk on Cross-Fertilization——

AUGUSTA. Won't someone exterminate him?

ALAN. *(Is* L. *of table—to* OLIVER) Turn your head to the right—that helps, sometimes—— *(*OLIVER *does so, but without avail. He grows more and more nervous.)*

MRS. WINSLOW. *(Sits—chair* R. *of* T.*)* What was the gist of it?

OLIVER. *(Draws the chair* L. *of table forward. Sits facing* MRS. WINSLOW. *Hoarsely)* Progress —town's industrial development—more factories—more business.

AUGUSTA. Mark can give an extemporaneous one!

OLIVER. *(Eagerly)* Yes! Yes, Mark—you're clever—— *(The band has just arrived and is playing* F.F.*)*

MARK. *(Very scared)* D—don't be silly . . . *(Turns away to above* L. *of* H. *The band-music stops suddenly. A voice is heard off left.)*

VOICE. Three cheers for the Winslows! *(*ALAN *crosses above table to* U.L. *of* H.*)*

CROWD. Hurrah! Hurrah! Hurrah! *(The cheers are followed by a pandemonium of noises, tin horns, wooden clappers, cow bells—shots from a repeating revolver, fire crackers—all the customary noises. Then comes an expectant hush.)*

(CHEERS.)

AUGUSTA. Oh, agony, agony! Oliver, go and tell them *something!* *(*OLIVER *does not budge. She speaks scornfully)* Head of the family—*you.* *(*OLIVER *takes a deep breath.)*

MRS. WINSLOW. *(Mumbles)* Friends—— On this auspicious occasion—— (OLIVER *rises.) Brave* boy.

*(*OLIVER *takes a deep breath and crosses to the railing. There is a shout followed by the silence. The family wait, anxious and helpless.* AUGUSTA *hands him one of the pieces. He takes it,*

then glares at her, throws it down. MARK *to below* R. *of* MRS. WINSLOW. *Band plays "He's a Jolly Good Fellow.")*

OLIVER. *(In a quavering voice)* "F-friends, we welcome you." *(He clears his throat.)* "This auspicious occasion may introduce to a city—a city—" *(His voice dwindles.)* "—even richer in—public spirit—citizens—" *(A pause; he repeats.)* "—uh —richer—uh—public spirit citizens——" *(A dreadful wait, the family suffers tortures. Someone in the crowd laughs mockingly. Others emit loud "sh-sh"-ses. Another silence. Again the jeer.)*

MARK. *(Below* R. *of* MRS. WINSLOW. *In a whisper)* Lord—what'll they think of us?

AUGUSTA. It's a disgrace. Next year they'll go to the Aldens. *(Sits chair above* T.*)*

MRS. WINSLOW. Why does he wait so long?

OLIVER. *(Doggedly)* "—richer—public spirit—uh—citizens——" *(There is another awful pause. Suddenly* RICHARD *crosses and stands beside* OLIVER. *Murmurs in the crowd.)*

RICHARD. *(To the crowd)* Hello, here I am. *I* am Richard—and I thank my brother for the flattering introduction as "public-spirited" citizen. *(Slaps* OLIVER *on shoulder.* OLIVER *to* L.C.5.) That's just the word for me—"public-spirited." *(He swallows hard and tries to control his trembling.)*

MRS. WINSLOW. *(To* MARK*)* His left knee—it's shaking so.

RICHARD. It applies to everything about me but my left knee, which at present's got private qualms. *(Takes drink of water. The crowd laughs.* OLIVER *crosses away from him to* U.V.L. RICHARD *takes heart from the laughter.)* My text this morning—my text is—— *(In panic, he looks at* OLIVER *for assistance.* OLIVER *compresses his lips and turns away.)*

ALAN. *(In a hoarse whisper above* R. *of* T.*)* Chamber of Commerce stuff.

MARK. *(In a hoarse whisper over* R. *of* T.*)* More factories! Industrial progress!

RICHARD. *(To the crowd)* "Industrial progress." *(A pause.)* And how silly it is. *(The crowd laughs again.)*

MARK. More factories—did you hear me? More factories.

RICHARD. *(On the table)* —No more factories under *any* circumstances!—And as for that pin factory of mine, every Saturday give workers full holiday to *forget* the old pins and enjoy themselves.

(Cheers of joy from the crowd. Band plays "He's a Jolly Good Fellow.")

MARK. Till September, you brat—only till September!

RICHARD. *(To the crowd)* —Not only till September! All the whole year round! *(More cheers.)* What the world needs is more leisure 'n' fewer alarm-clocks—less do-as-you're-told 'n' more do-as-you-please. As—as the immortal patriot, poet—er—poet patriot—Cap'n—Cap'n John Keats said, in—in—his third epistle to the Indians, "Beauty is Truth," 'n' vice versa. So why fuss 'n' fume trying to cross-fertilize a beautiful town like this into something it was never intended to be? It's all right as it is. Too much of this making things over, anyway. "Industrial center"—— Bah! All smoke 'n' steam 'n' scurry 'n' scamper. Don't do it! Stay different! Let it be! *(He turns to the family and says lowly)* —And you let *me* be.

(WARN Curtain.)
(MURMURS.)

OLIVER. *(To* R. *of chair above* T.*)* Get through

See page 82

with this nonsense, my friend—I've got something waiting for you.

RICHARD. *(To the crowd)* When we get through with this nonsense, my friends, we've got something waiting for us——(OLIVER, *hand to head, goes into house)*—the satisfaction of knowing that to be different doesn't mean to be inferior. There's no such thing as inferiority, anyway—neither in individuals, nor in towns, nor in nations. This little nation realized that once in 1776—and you know what happened—— *(Cheers from the crowd.* RICHARD *turns to the family with an expression which says "That'll get 'em." To the crowd)* —Being different—*that's* what makes life worth *living!* America's kept *her* individuality—where'd she be if she hadn't? Let's keep ours!—And let's see this inferiority thing as the myth it is—a myth—invented by tyrants—to make *themselves superior! (The crowd is hushed.)* And oh, my dear, *dear* fellow-citizens, if any one of *you* feels it, mind you treat it just the way those inferior little Colonies did: declare yourself—free, equal—and independent! Don't fire until you see the whites of their eyes. *But* when you do see 'em, *black 'em!*

(The crowd breaks into a pandemonium of shouts—"Yea! Yea! Yea!" OLIVER *enters window* U.R.*—comes to* U.R. *of* H.)

MUFF. *(Her shrill voice demanding, off* L.*)* What's the matter with Richard? *(The crowd roars a response—"He's all right!")*

NANCY. *(Off* L.*—shouts)* Three cheers for Richard Winslow!

(The answering murmurs are deafening. RICHARD *still on the table, bows to crowd. The murmurs of crowd continue until curtain.* MARK *has*

taken a cigarette from his pocket and lighted it. RICHARD *crosses front to* R. *of hammock.* MRS. WINSLOW *sits, chair* L. AUGUSTA *stands above her.)*

RICHARD. Now we are equals or not?

OLIVER. *(At* U.R. *of* H.*)* You'll see what we are soon enough. You're going to start——

RICHARD. *(*R. *of hammock)* Now, as I started to tell you: I *own* this house——

OLIVER. Nonsense!

RICHARD. And I *own* the factory! And everything else you've got, and more too!

OLIVER. Don't talk like an idiot!

RICHARD. If you don't believe me, ask Alan.

OLIVER. Oh—Alan! (OLIVER, *above the* R. *of hammock, exclaims impatiently, goes up* R. MARK, *in front of hammock, exclaims impatiently, "Agh!" Sits* R. *side of hammock. Puts the cigarette in his mouth.)*

RICHARD. You can go to Alan for all the morbid details.

(ALAN *goes to* L. *of hammock.* NANCY *enters from garden on* L. *Crosses to upper* R. *of hammock.)*

ALAN. *(At* L. *of hammock)* If anyone wants me, I may be found in my room. *(Exits window up* L. OLIVER *paces down* R.C., *then up again, then down.)*

RICHARD. *(At* R. *of hammock)* Hello, Nancy! 'Been a hot morning. *(Plucks the cigarette from* MARK'S *mouth. Goes to* NANCY.) Swim? (OLIVER *is a little below* R. *of* RICHARD.)

NANCY. *(Above the* L. *of hammock)* I'd love it.

RICHARD. If anyone wants me, I may be found in *my pool.*

(The band strikes up with "Dixie," F.F. RICHARD *touches the cigarette to the three balloons on the* R. *side of hammock, he and* NANCY *crossing to garden on* L. *The family are staring after them.)*

CURTAIN

ACT III

SCENE: *The living-room.*

TIME: *A few hours later.*

AT RISE: *The stage is empty. Then* NANCY *enters from French window* U.R., *wearing the same dress as in Act II. She is followed by* RICHARD, *who nows wears a dark coat, gray trousers and a flower in his buttonhole.*

RICHARD. *(At upper* L. *of piano)* Nancy! Wasn't it great? Good swim, eh?

NANCY. *(To* R. *of sofa)* Marvelous! I'm so cool——

RICHARD. *(Advancing to* C.3) Nancy—— *(She looks up inquiringly. He concludes lamely)* Hello.

NANCY. How are you?

RICHARD. I'm wonderful! I'd like to pull the sun out of the sky! I'd like to have great dripping chunks of it on bread, like yellow honey.

NANCY. Well, why don't you?

RICHARD. Would you like some?

NANCY. I'd love it. *(Goes to sofa, sits lower end. She smiles and nods. He strides to the French window,* U.R., *flings it open and shakes his finger at the sun.)*

RICHARD. Mind your manners, you fat rascal, or I shall have you down and eat you. *(He comes in.)*

NANCY. Didn't you get any?

RICHARD. *(At* L. *of piano)* A little. Here, catch. (NANCY *holds both hands out and catches, then raises her cupped hands to her mouth and makes a sound of tasting.)*

NANCY. Oh, nice! *(A pause. Her hands sink down slowly and she looks at him, smiling tenderly, perhaps a little pityingly.)*

RICHARD. Nancy——

NANCY. What?

RICHARD. Don't move.

NANCY. Why?

RICHARD. You look so beautiful.

NANCY. I wish I were.

RICHARD. *(Crosses a few steps toward her and stops)* I shan't ever forget you sitting there now.

NANCY. How do you know you won't?

RICHARD. *(Goes to her)* I know, because in a Japanese poem a woman dusts a window shutter ever so carefully to keep the shadow of a pine tree quite perfect on it. So I can dust what remembers things, to take this image of you clear and deep. *(Takes out handkerchief, opens his coat and dusts over his heart.)* See? It's dusted. You know, I don't believe you just happened the way ordinary people do. You're—the strangeness about you—as if all the lovely things on earth were gathered and pruned and ordered—and then a picture painted from them. You're the picture come to life. Or I might be imagining you—I feel as though you're someone I dreamt—— If I woke——

NANCY. I'm real, all right—never you fear. I'm alive.

RICHARD. Let's see . . . *(He holds out his hands to her, palms upward. She places hers upon them. Speaks in a hushed voice)* Yes,—— *(She rises slowly.)* I can feel you're alive. It's like a lake looks, with rain falling on it. Oh, Nancy dear, dear Nancy, you feel it too, don't you? What is it? What is it? (ALAN *appears in the window up* R.)

NANCY. *(Recovering herself)* What am I thinking of? *(Crosses front of table* R.C. *and exits door* R. ALAN *comes down* R. *of piano and closes the door.)*

ALAN. *(*R. *of piano)* Richard, I'd be careful of Nancy if I were you.

RICHARD. *(At* L. *of piano)* Careful?

ALAN. She suffers from a complaint known as over-enthusiasm.

RICHARD. Over enth—what do you mean——

ALAN. You'd better skip, Richard. The family's been rowing like magpies for two hours in Noll's room. They're coming down in a minute.

RICHARD. 'Like to hear them.

ALAN. I'll call you later on. It'll be better, really.

RICHARD. *(Hesitates)* Well, you're my lawyer—but I'll be back. *(He exits window up* R. ALAN *crosses above to* L. *of piano.* AUGUSTA, MARK, OLIVER, MUFF *enter from door* R.*)*

MARK. *(Still off, as he comes in)* Well, of all the rotten, low-down ways to take a mean advantage—— *(To above the piano.)*

AUGUSTA. *(Through* MARK'S *speech—crosses front, sits on stool* R.C.*)* It's outrageous. Simply outrageous. Whoever heard of such a thing!

OLIVER. *(At* R. *of piano, shaking his finger at* ALAN*)* An insult to Father's memory, that's what it is!

MARK. *(At* ALAN*)* Of course it's an insult to Father's memory—Grandfather's, too. *(Closes the door.)*

(ALAN *crosses to sofa at* L. OLIVER *is crossing below the piano to* U.R. *of sofa.* MRS. WINSLOW *enters from the dining-room, crossing to armchair* C.*)*

MRS. WINSLOW. Children! Children! *(Sits, armchair* C.*)*

OLIVER. *(To* ALAN *at sofa)* It's amazing to me how a sane person could even contemplate such a trick.

MARK. *(Coming down* R. *of piano)* We've got no proof that he's sane.

MUFF. *(Front of piano)* Heavens, what a racket! *(Crosses, sits, sofa.* ALAN *crosses to* L. *of piano.)*

OLIVER. *(To* MRS. WINSLOW) If he hadn't been brought up with so much care, you might expect it. But when——

MRS. WINSLOW. Richard has always been a little weak on right and wrong.

MARK. *(To* ALAN, *who is at* L. *of piano)* Well, why don't you say something?

ALAN. *(*L. *of piano)* I've been waiting since the crowd left for a lull in the conversation.

MARK. Oh, come down off your high horse.

OLIVER. *(*L. *of* MRS. WINSLOW, *patting her)* Don't worry, Mother. We'll arrange it. *(To* ALAN) Are you sure that Transfer of Rights is complete enough? (ALAN *shuts his lips tightly—goes up* R.C.*)*

AUGUSTA. Alan! Do you realize it's nearly dinner-time?

ALAN. The statute—the law—of New York state says that——

MARK. (R. *of piano)* Dumbest nonsense I ever heard of——

OLIVER. Mark! (ALAN *glares at him—then goes up* R.C.*)*

MARK. Or why didn't they find it out when the thing was probated?

OLIVER. Mark! (MARK *sits armchair* R.*)*

MRS. WINSLOW. Surely old Judge Morris was competent to——

AUGUSTA. Mother, it's common knowledge what

killed that man—— (ALAN *to* L. *of piano, opening books.)*

MUFF. *(Glumly)* It's drink done it!

OLIVER. *(*L. *of* C.3, *to* ALAN) Supposing it had been discovered, then? (ALAN *does not answer.* OLIVER *roars)* I'm speaking to you!

ALAN. *(*L. *of* S.*)* Dear, dear.

AUGUSTA. *(Pleading)* Alan——!

MRS. WINSLOW. Do you realize that Oliver is speaking to you?

ALAN. It would have been Mrs. Winslow's duty as executrix to see that a guardian was appointed, and his share at once placed in safe keeping.

MARK. But confound it! Some of it was tied up in the business!

ALAN. Such risks are not countenanced—she'd have been compelled to take it out within a year—close down the factory and liquidate.

AUGUSTA. *(Rising)* Preposterous.

ALAN. My dear, I am quoting law—— (AUGUSTA *stops* C., *glares at him—"You know about law!")*—not poetry! (AUGUSTA *crosses front of sofa up* L. *Sits stool,* R.C. *to* OLIVER.) What did Judge Ainslee tell you when you 'phoned?

OLIVER. *(*C.3.*)* I merely asked his opinion on—on—a hypothetical case.

ALAN. And he said your hypothetical family wouldn't have a hypothetical leg to stand on, didn't he? And that their one chance was to conciliate the brat—— *(A pause.)*

MARK. *(Rising, crosses to above stool* R.C., *watching* ALAN) I don't believe Richard would have done it without someone's pretty strong encouragement. *(Continues to above piano; comes down* R. *of it.)*

ALAN. *(Rising)* Oh, believe what you like. *(To* OLIVER) The only question now is, how much you'll still owe him over and above what you've now got.

OLIVER. *(Grunts)* Eh?

ALAN. *(To below* R. *of* W.T. OLIVER *to below* L. *of* MRS. WINSLOW. *To* MRS. WINSLOW) However you figure it, he's entitled to a sum which comes —as I've repeatedly told you—to more, considerably more, than the whole estate is now worth.

MRS. WINSLOW. *(Sitting armchair* C.) There must be some way——

ALAN. There's—just one . . . *(All look hopeful.)* You could disprove his legitimacy.

MUFF. Eh?

MRS. WINSLOW. It's awful—the whole thing is simply awful.

AUGUSTA. *(To* L. *of* MRS. WINSLOW) Don't notice him, mother.

MRS. WINSLOW. How sharper than a serpent's tooth.

ALAN. *(*R. *of* W.T.*)* Not at all. And I've no doubt that eventually he'll come around—compromise, at any rate. That is, if you behave——

MARK. *(To* R. *of stool)* If we what?

ALAN. Behave, I said. Believe me, it's in your own best interests to make any concessions necessary. If you don't—— Well, he's worked out some plan or other—I've an idea you wouldn't like the taste of it. I'll get him. (ALAN *exits, window* B.R.)

(MUFF *rises, laughs, crosses front to door* L. MARK *above* OLIVER, *crosses to sofa, sits upper end.* OLIVER *crosses in step with* MARK, *sits below* MARK *on sofa.* AUGUSTA *to mantel* U.L.C. *The family sit motionless for a while.)*

MARK. There may be something in what he says.

Noll. (AUGUSTA *crosses above armchair* C. *to* L. *of piano.)*

OLIVER. Yes, I believe Richard will ultimately do what is right.

MARK. He's never been one to take a petty advantage.

MRS. WINSLOW. It is quite unlike his sweet, retiring nature.

MUFF. *(Sits bench* L.*)* Well, upon my soul——

AUGUSTA. Isn't it lovely?

MUFF. *(In a hollow voice)* How the old home has changed. *(They glare at* MUFF.)

AUGUSTA. Everything we own stolen right from under our noses—and you sit there—holding your chins—sentimentalizing—over Richard's noble qualities—Richard's! (MARK *and* OLIVER *self-consciously uncup their chins.* AUGUSTA *to* R.C.2, *continuing scornfully)* —The little tin god—kow-tow to him—do! *(Turns up* R.C.*)*

MARK. If you'd quit stewing like a tin kettle and use your tin head, you'd understand that if Richard chooses to be nasty——

AUGUSTA. *(Crossing to them—mockingly)* If he chooses to be nasty! Dear, dear! *(Crossing to* OLIVER) Don't you realize that giving in to him only makes him all the cockier? *(A pause.)*

MARK. *(To* OLIVER) There may be something in what she says.

MUFF. You learned, didn't you, Mark?

AUGUSTA. He simply battens on kindness! Can't you see that what he wants is the soundest drubbing he's ever got? Then, if that doesn't work, there'll be time enough for concessions. (MARK *looks at* OLIVER, *moves toward him.* OLIVER *looks at* MARK, *moves toward him.)*

MARK. *(To* OLIVER) You know, I think she's right. *(Pats her arm.)* You're right.

OLIVER. Yes—it's discipline he needs—— *(Pats her arm.)* You're right—just as Nancy said——

MARK. *(Puzzled)* "Just as Nancy——" *(Quickly)* What did Nancy say?

OLIVER. Oh—— (RICHARD *is heard off* R., *calling and whistling to Portly.)*

MUFF. Shh—shhh!

AUGUSTA. Now land on him—hear me? Hard! (RICHARD *enters back right with Portly in his arms and a flower in his buttonhole.* AUGUSTA *crosses to stool* R.C.*)* My! Aren't we dressed up, though? *(Sits stool* R.C.*)*

RICHARD. *(*R. *of* C.3) It's a failing of the nouveau riche—— *(Waggles the puppy's paw at* AUGUSTA.)

MUFF. Richard, what I want to know is—are you legitimate? (RICHARD *laughs, then looks around him at the family.)*

RICHARD. *(To* R. *of upper end of sofa)* Are you all comfortable? Quite comfortable?

MARK. What's that to you?

RICHARD. I always like my guests to be comfortable. *(Turns up* L. *of* MRS. WINSLOW.)

MRS. WINSLOW. *(Indicating the puppy)* Put him outside, Richard.

RICHARD. I—— He's not hurting anything.

MRS. WINSLOW. This instant!

MARK. *(Rising)* Do as you're told——!

(RICHARD *hesitates a little, weakening.* ALAN *comes in, window up* R., *to* L. *of piano.)*

AUGUSTA. He'll be wanting him in the dining-room next.

MRS. WINSLOW. The dining-room, indeed! Richard, please. (RICHARD *slowly crosses and places the puppy on the porch, window* U.L.) Now run along and find a beetle—— (AUGUSTA *smiles at the family and says, "See?" inaudibly.* RICHARD *returns and seats himself in* OLIVER'S *chair.* OLIVER *rises*—U.R. *of sofa—and stands towering over him.)*

OLIVER. Get out of that chair! (RICHARD *does not move.)*

MRS. WINSLOW. Do as Oliver says!

MARK. *(Above sofa)* Go on—move!

MUFF. Don't make yourself impossible, Richard. (RICHARD *hesitates, looks at* ALAN.)

ALAN. Why battle over a chair? (RICHARD *hesitates.)*

OLIVER. *(At* L. *of piano)* Will you get out? (RICHARD *rises reluctantly.)*

RICHARD. Well—guess one's as good as another. (OLIVER *seats himself at the desk.* RICHARD *crosses front and seats himself on sofa.)*

OLIVER. Stand up! (RICHARD *reluctantly obeys.* OLIVER *takes a long paper from his pocket.)* Now this nonsense of yours is going to stop where it is.

MUFF. It's funny, all right—but a joke's a joke, Richard.

MRS. WINSLOW. Funny? It's an insult to his father's memory!

MARK. Ungrateful little brat——

RICHARD. *(To her left)* Mother, I—you won't suffer a bit from it. I——

MARK. Be quiet and listen!

OLIVER. We're going to put a stop to this, once and for all. Here—— *(He hands him the paper.)* That's what's called a "Transfer of Rights"—— (RICHARD *opens the paper.)* You haven't a right in the world, understand—but to avoid any further trouble for yourself—you sign there at the bottom—where I've put the cross—— (MARK *hands him his fountain-pen.)*

MARK. Here—— (RICHARD *takes it. He*

frowns over the paper.) Go ahead, now—we haven't all day——

RICHARD. Wait'll I read it, will you?

MARK. You can read it afterward——

RICHARD. *(Feebly)* I'm—I'm not going to sign anything I haven't read—— *(He glances warily at* ALAN *at* L. *of piano, who shakes his head.)*

AUGUSTA. Alan, you keep out—— (RICHARD *stares fixedly at the paper.* OLIVER *rises.)*

OLIVER. *(Thundering)* Will you put your name there or won't you?

MARK. Say, must I——?

OLIVER. Sign it!

MARK. Go on. Write! (RICHARD *places his paper on the sofa, and with trembling fingers poises the pen to write.* AUGUSTA *smiles triumphantly.)*

MRS. WINSLOW. Well—that's better——

MARK. Thought you'd gouge your own mother, did you? How'd you like your friend Nancy to know that? *(At* NANCY'S *name,* RICHARD *stiffens, then looks at* MARK *defiantly.)*

RICHARD. How'd you like to tell her?

OLIVER. Sign that! (RICHARD *turns on him.)*

RICHARD. Who says to sign it?

OLIVER. I do——

MARK. We all do!

RICHARD. You can all go jump in the lake! (MRS. WINSLOW *gasps. Crossing* L. *of* MRS. WINSLOW) All but you, Mother—you needn't.

MUFF. That's the time your foot slipped, Mark. (MARK'S *eyes narrow.)*

MARK. *(To* U.R. *of sofa)* I'm getting a line on this now. (OLIVER *comes charging around above sofa, to* L. *of* RICHARD.)

OLIVER. Will you sign that paper or won't you?

RICHARD. *No! (Tears the paper in half.)* And if you mention it again, I'll make you eat it. *(Sticks a piece in the breast pocket of both* MARK *and*

OLIVER *as he does so.)* There's your share, and yours! *(He crosses above to the desk, and seats himself again in* OLIVER'S *chair.* MARK *at* R. *of sofa.)* Now, when you're ready to listen, I've got a few interesting remarks to make—— *(There is a fuming silence.* RICHARD *straightens out the top of the desk to give himself elbow-room.* OLIVER *whispers something to* MARK. MARK—*"Sure—yep."* OLIVER *clears his throat.)*

OLIVER. If we've been——

MARK. *(Simultaneously)* Perhaps we've been— (OLIVER *glares at* MARK. MARK *subsides.)*

OLIVER. If we haven't shown the proper consideration for your ideas of a career—— *(Above sofa.)* Of course we're willing to make a few concessions— (MARK *rolls the piece of paper in his hands.)*

AUGUSTA. Oliver, you're—— *(He ignores her objection.)*

OLIVER. *(Crossing above to* L. *of* T.*)* You can have your allowance and a regular room to yourself—— (ALAN *crosses above armchair* C. *to* L.C.*)*

MARK. Provided, of course, that you'll be reasonable about this—— (MARK *is rolling the piece of paper between his hands.)*

RICHARD. Don't do that!

MUFF. It's what you've been begging for, all along, isn't it? *(Another pause.)*

MARK. What more do you want?

ALAN. *(To above sofa)* I'm sure the family would live up to their side of it, Richard.

OLIVER. Yes, yes——

RICHARD. *(Suddenly)* They'll live up to my side of it! Whose lawyer are you, anyway?

ALAN. Why—uh—yours, I suppose.

RICHARD. Well, you're fired. *(He opens the large checkbook on the table.)* As to the family finances, henceforth I shall sign all checks myself.

(He begins to make one out.) I'll expect a thousand cash-advance in the bank by tomorrow.

MARK. *(To* L. *of spinet)* It's a hold-up!

OLIVER. *(*L. *of* T.*)* If you think we're going to stand for this!

RICHARD. Listen! If I have to bring public suit for these rights of mine——

MRS. WINSLOW. *(Rising)* Richard! Oh—what would people think? No one must know—not one soul, children! Not one soul! *(She sinks into armchair again.* OLIVER *crosses above sofa to* L. *of* MRS. WINSLOW. MARK *comes to* R. *of* MRS. WINSLOW. *They comfort her.* ALAN *goes to bookcase up* L.C.*)*

RICHARD. *(Tearing off check)* That's up to all of you. There—check number one—Scribner's—forty-two dollars—— *(He holds it up to view, smiling with satisfaction upon it. Again* MARK'S *eyes narrow.* RICHARD *places the check in an envelope which already contains a letter and seals it. Then he makes out more checks.)* Provided a disagreeable lawsuit's not necessary, I'm willing, as head of the family, to make a few concessions. First of all, there'll be a generous life income for Mother. Then maybe later on I'll settle a couple of dollars on each of you—I don't know—— You can count on a dowry, Muff——

MUFF. *(Sitting bench* L.*)* Oh—let that get noised around a bit, will you?

RICHARD. For the duration of good behavior, I'll even continue your allowances. And by "good behavior" I mean the fulfillment of certain conditions I'm about to make.

MARK. *(Crossing to* R. *of sofa—between his teeth)* Isn't it rich? (OLIVER *to* U.R. *of sofa.)*

RICHARD. *(To* MARK) From you, Mark and Oliver, I shall expect weekly, till further notice, the contribution of an original short story, poem or essay which you can write in the evenings.

OLIVER. *(To* U.R. *of sofa)* Hah!

MARK. I'll write him a poem——

RICHARD. Good! I'll be glad to criticize it personally. (MARK *to* L.R. *of sofa.)*

OLIVER. *(At* U.R. *of sofa)* We're to follow your orders to the letter, are we?

RICHARD. You certainly are. And one of 'em's that you're not to talk business at meals.

OLIVER. I'm not, eh?

RICHARD. No. It bores me. (OLIVER *sits upper end of sofa.)* Just bear in mind that you're not major-general here now—you're buck private. Also, please remember that my rooms are *my rooms.* I'll choose a few tomorrow.

AUGUSTA. *(Sitting stool* R.C.*)* Such a large choice, isn't there?

RICHARD. *(Rising, gathers up the checks)* It'll be larger—'cause you see on Monday you and Alan move to the house at Grand View.

OLIVER. *(Rising)* That's been sold.

RICHARD. I don't recall selling it. (MARK *goes up* L.C. OLIVER *crosses, goes out onto porch, window* R.*)*

AUGUSTA. Catch me living in that shanty!

ALAN. *(At* B.C.*)* I'm afraid you'll have to, my dear.

RICHARD. *(To* ALAN) I'm afraid she will, too. *(To* ALAN) Now you're paid off. . . . *(He crosses to* MRS. WINSLOW. AUGUSTA, *disgusted, turns facing* R.*)* Here's your check, Mother. *(She accepts it uncertainly.)*

MRS. WINSLOW. Th—thank you, dear boy. (RICHARD *returns toward the table.* MARK *holds out his hand as he comes to him.)*

RICHARD. *(As he passes* MARK) Kindly wait your turn. *(Continues to above the table.)* Muff— (OLIVER *comes down* R. *of piano.* MUFF *takes the check and reads it.)*

MUFF. Whee! Now I can go straight! *(Then suddenly worried)* Is it good?

OLIVER. *(At* R. *of piano)* No!

RICHARD. *(Above sofa)* Yes! (OLIVER *goes out onto porch.)* Now, Lord Chesterfield.—Beau Brummel—— (RICHARD *offers check to* MARK. MARK *grabs at it. Deftly recovers it.)* Ah! Papa spank! *(And offers it again very formally.* MARK *accepts it.* RICHARD *crosses to* R. *of* AUGUSTA *and gives her a check.)* Augusta.

AUGUSTA. *(Sitting on stool* R.C., *facing* R., *rising)* Really, you're too good. *(Goes up to bookcase* R.C. *Without a word,* RICHARD *lays a check on the piano for* OLIVER, *sees he is out on the porch and whistles at him to attract his attention.* RICHARD *crosses to above sofa.* OLIVER *comes down* L. *of piano, grabs the check, tears it in pieces, throws them on piano as he goes to above the stool* R.C.)

OLIVER. *(To* RICHARD—*is above the stool)* Get clear on one thing: When this is finally settled—as it will be—you'll work off every cent of your debt in the factory. *(Sits stool* R.C.—RICHARD *regards him speculatively.)*

RICHARD. *(At* U.R. *of sofa)* Oliver, there's something so dreadfully thick about you. *(To* MUFF) Haven't you often felt it?

MUFF. Often.

RICHARD. Old Rock of Ages. No mind, no wit, just the ten commandments, and a deep, chesty voice. (OLIVER *rises.)*

MUFF. Boom! Boom!

MRS. WINSLOW. Hush, Martha. Richard is speaking! (OLIVER *looks at his mother, stunned, again sits, stool* R.C. MUFF *smothers her laugh and turns away.)*

RICHARD. *(Goes to his* L.) You weren't born to rule people. Your eye's too straight for it. A born ruler's got to be just a trifle cock-eyed, so's to see both sides of things. (OLIVER *turns on the stool, facing up stage.* RICHARD *goes above him.)* You'll never be able to see my side, but I'll do my own work in my own way, Noll——

OLIVER. Oh, will you?

RICHARD. Yes. And even if I fail at it, I'll still be ahead of you—'cause I move, Noll, and you—— *(To* MUFF, *crossing to above the sofa)* Well, look at him—"Old Sitting Bull"! *(Crosses to above the table* L., *commences to whistle loudly "Home Sweet Home."* MRS. WINSLOW *rises, draws a deep breath and, crossing above the table* L., *exits into the dining-room.* MARK *passes up and down* R. *of sofa.* OLIVER *rises, goes up to the window up* R.*)* Now, then, where's a stamp? Where's a stamp? *(He searches the drawer of desk and* OLIVER *sits armchair, front of piano.* RICHARD *finally finds a stamp and affixes it to the Scribner's letter.* MARK *is pacing up and down* R. *of the sofa. Comes to* U.R. *of sofa.* RICHARD *is standing at* U.L. *of the sofa. Smiles at* MARK'S *threatening attitude.)* What's the matter, Mark? You don't look very happy. (MARK *at* U.R. *of sofa, reaches over and gives* RICHARD'S *nose a good sound pulling.* OLIVER *rises—to* R. *of piano.* RICHARD *sniffs it back into shape and cries)* Disrespect to the royal nose! Mark's allowance cut in half! (OLIVER *quickly goes out the window up* R. MARK *goes to armchair* C., *sits.* ALAN *crosses above the chair to* R. *of* W.T.*)*

AUGUSTA. *(To above the piano)* Alan, will you come, please? (ALAN *starts to go.)*

RICHARD. *(Sitting chair above table* L.*—holds out the letter)* Alan! Post this, will you? (ALAN *hesitating.)* Better step, son, better step. (AUGUSTA *exits window up* R. ALAN *smiles, crosses and takes the letter, then recrosses and exits window* *up* R.*)* Where's Nancy? *(Reaches over the table and pushes* MUFF.) I want to see Nancy.

MARK. *(Rising, to* U.R. *of sofa)* I'd like to see her for a moment myself.

MUFF. Popular girl, Nancy. *(Gives* RICHARD *her check.)* When you find her, give her this, will you? Say it's from me, on account.

MARK. She wins, eh?

MUFF. *(Rising, from bench at* L., *crossing to* U.L. *of piano)* She certainly does.

MARK. *(To* RICHARD) I just want to inform you that I'm able to put two and two together.

RICHARD. That's fine, Mark. *(To* MUFF) He can count.

MUFF. But he doesn't seem to, does he? At least, not with Nancy. *(Laughs and goes out window up* R. MARK *studies him for a moment, then laughs shortly.* RICHARD *starts.)*

MARK. *(*R. *of sofa)* Quite irresistible, aren't you?

RICHARD. *(Sitting armchair above* T.L.*)* I'm a gilded youth, Mark. Just a gilded youth.

MARK. Besides your highwayman talents, quite the young ladykiller, too.

RICHARD. Better run along now, Mark. I'm busy——

MARK. I suppose you think she's a prize little accomplice, eh? Well, let me tell you it's you who's the accomplice.

RICHARD. What the devil are you talking about?

MARK. Only the truth. *(In mock compassion)* Aw—and did he think he was such a fascinating fellow? And did he think she fell head over heels at first sight— Pity to disillusion the little man.

RICHARD. Liar!

MARK. Why, she had a regular formula—— *(He laughs mockingly.)* His trouble is mental—be kind to him, Mark—it may make a man of him.

Then to Noll: Lock up his silly books and manuscripts—that'll make him a business man!!!

(WARN Bell.)

RICHARD. Oh, shut up——

MARK. Oh, Lord knows what she wanted—but she's sharpened her wits on the lot of us, all right. Interested in you? Baah! She's interested in herself. She glories in the way she can manage people. It's her main amusement. (ALAN *enters* U.U.R.) When you've seen as much of the world as I have, my son, you'll learn to recognize that type of woman by the look in her eye. (ALAN *at* L. *of piano.)*

RICHARD. *(Rising)* You damned liar you—get out——

MARK. Ask Muff, then. Didn't you hear what Muff said about that check? "Tell her it's from me on account."

ALAN. *(At* L. *of piano)* Mark——

MARK. Shut up! *(To* U.R. *of sofa)* And do you know what for? A bet, that's what! Fifty dollars she could get some spunk into you in a week. Flatter it in. Honestly, with people like you to experiment on, life looks a lot brighter for the guinea pig. *(He crosses to window up* R.*)* But I'll tell her a few things about teaching babies to steal.

ALAN. She never dreamed he'd actually do this.

MARK. No? Let's see what she says.

(He goes out, window up R. RICHARD *looks at* ALAN, *almost too overcome to speak. Then.)*

RICHARD. *(At* U.L. *of sofa)* Oh, I knew the bottom would fall out of it somehow. I knew.

ALAN. *(Crosses to* R. *of sofa)* Most of that was nothing but Mark's talk.

RICHARD. I heard what Muff said. She did bet with Muff, didn't she?

ALAN. Why—uh——

RICHARD. Oh, that's a rotten trick. *(Comes down to* L. *of* L.L. *of sofa.)*

ALAN. She wanted to help you.

RICHARD. Whatever she wanted, she was with the rest of them. Using me, meddling, making me over—always making me over.

ALAN. You're taking this too hard, you really are.

RICHARD. Anyone but her, Alan—anyone. It's humiliating enough, when your own family treats you like a worm, but when someone—someone you thought—liked you, thinks you're so low and pitiful that you've got to be bucked up with kindness.—Oh, that's—that's awful. She couldn't ever do anything but pity me.

ALAN. Richard, I think she's honestly fond of you.

RICHARD. *(Crosses to* L. *of piano)* So'm I fond of Portly: I nursed him through distemper.

ALAN. You must have been a little more than a sick dog to her, or——

RICHARD. *(Sits armchair up* C.*)* Oh, but Alan—It's such a long way from someone who's always been adored to—someone who's always—been despised——

ALAN. *(To his* L.*)* But you haven't——

RICHARD. *(Quickly)* Yes, I have! But I'm myself, just the same—and she's herself! It's other people who've put one here and one—*(He gestures helplessly into the air)*—there.— *(A pause.)* Still, there must be some place to meet in between, as ourselves, Alan. There's got to be some place, hasn't there, Alan? *(*ALAN *does not answer.)* One can go up, and the other can come down.—— *(A pause. His voice rises, suddenly)* The other can be brought down. She's got to be, Alan. She's got to realize that we're equals. Else, else . . .

ALAN. Else what?

RICHARD. Else she's lost to me.

(He rises, and leans on mantel. ALAN *goes to sofa.* KATIE *crosses from dining-room to hall.)*

KATIE. Dinner is served, Mr. Richard.

(She goes out window up R. NANCY *enters from hall.* RICHARD *sees her and at once occupies himself with setting the clock.* ALAN *crosses to* L. *of piano.)*

NANCY. *(*L.R. *of piano)* Alan, Mark says that——

ALAN. Exactly.—And even you couldn't ask for a tighter tight corner. Good luck to you.

*(*ALAN *goes out window up* R. RICHARD *sets the clock. It strikes five-thirty. He moves the hand to six.)*

NANCY. *(Suddenly)* Richard, I—— *(The clock strikes six. She stops.* RICHARD *moves it to six-thirty.)*

RICHARD. What?—— *(It strikes six-thirty. He moves it to seven.)*

NANCY. I was going to say that—— *(It strikes seven.)* Oh-h-h-h-h-! *(She turns away, biting her lip.* RICHARD *moves the hand to twenty-seven minutes past seven, starts the clock, closes its door, and turns to* NANCY.*)*

RICHARD. Now; you were saying?

(She watches the clock, expecting another. AUGUSTA *and* OLIVER *enter and cross to the dining-room.)*

AUGUSTA. Dinner is ready. *(They go out.)*

NANCY. *(Above stool* R.C.*)* Richard—surely you

wouldn't misconstrue what—what nearly happened——

RICHARD. *(Coming down* C.*)* Of course not.

NANCY. And why not?

RICHARD. *(Smiles, turns away)* You are amusing—— *(To chair above* T.L.*)*

NANCY. *(Condemnatory)* Richard, I've heard what you've done to your family.

RICHARD. Have you, Nancy?

NANCY. Yes—and I presume in a way I'm responsible for it.

RICHARD. *(Innocently)* Why, how could you be?

NANCY. Of—of course you don't seriously intend keeping what you've taken.

RICHARD. Why not? It's mine. There's even a law about it.

NANCY. Law or no law, you're taking advantage of a petty technicality. *(Pleading)* Give it back—there's a lamb.

RICHARD. Sorry. Can't be a lamb any more. Been one too long.

NANCY. Well, in my opinion, it's simply rep—repre——

RICHARD. "Reprehensible"— *(Clock strikes 7:30)* —but I hate people without audacity, don't you?

NANCY. Your own family—

RICHARD. "A man's greatest victory——"

NANCY. You must have a heart of stone.

RICHARD. *(Lights match)* "I think to be great, you have to be remorseless. Every great man seems to be. When people oppose him, what does he do? Just simply extinguishes them." *(Blows out match.)*

NANCY. It's like you, to keep turning my own thoughtless words against me.—And I thought I was helping you—— *(She laughs, shortly)* Well——

*(*MUFF *enters from* U.R., *crosses* L.*)*

MUFF. Dinner's ready.

(She goes out into dining-room. NANCY *sits lower end of sofa.)*

RICHARD. *(To* L. *of sofa)* You did help me. And I'm grateful for that. I am grateful, Nancy.

NANCY. Then show it, by——

RICHARD. —But I didn't have any illusions about your motives.

NANCY. What's the matter with my motives?

RICHARD. They get mixed.

NANCY. Why, I——

RICHARD. *(Giving her check)* Here—it's from Muff—on account. Nancy, you made a sporting bet with Muff on an experiment that promised to amuse you. *(She turns away, shamefaced.)* Don't you think that was the main thing—and that helping me was just incidental?

NANCY. Incidental!

RICHARD. Yes. Truly.—Wasn't most of it for the fun you got—managing people—and the satisfaction you felt in being able to make someone over? Think, Nancy.

NANCY. You're telling me odd things about myself.

RICHARD. I'm telling you true things.

NANCY. Even so—the least I could do now would be to straighten out the mess I've made, wouldn't it?

RICHARD. And from what motive this time, do you know?

NANCY. I'd have to—in conscience—for the sake of your family.

RICHARD. No—for your sake. Your sake always. Your sake first. If someone else gains, it's the merest chance. That's too bad, but it's so.

NANCY. I—don't see it.

RICHARD. You want me to go back to what I was.

NANCY. *(Rising, steps backward to* C.2*)* No! No!

RICHARD. Yes, you do. Because all of a sudden you find that people and—and things have got out of your hands. That hurts your sense of superiority, doesn't it? Oh, I know what a terribly precious thing it is to you! So long as you've got it, nothing can touch you, can it?

NANCY. In other words, you think I'm a vain, empty little fool.

RICHARD. Oh, no, I'm not saying what I think of you. I'm just asking what it is you want of me.

NANCY. I don't know what I want.

(Goes to above stool R.C.*—*MARK *comes to window up* R.*, sees them, angrily crosses on porch to window up* L.*—Enter and exit into dining-room.* ALAN *follows* MARK. RICHARD *goes to her* L.*)*

RICHARD. Don't worry about their old money. Tomorrow, I'll give it back to them. *(She glances at him quickly. He smiles.)* I don't need a big stick to help keep my end up. I can keep it up alone. *(He smiles again.)* —Thanks to you.

NANCY. Thank them. Thank them for every moment of deviling they've given you. You ought to, you know. You really ought. You'll see that some day when—when you realize how—how nice it is to be like you and how awful it is to be—like me.

RICHARD. *(Takes her hand)* Oh, Nancy, Nancy! Must you be superior? Isn't being equal enough? *(She averts her head.)* —Or are you afraid something might happen to spoil all your beautiful contentment—something even as humiliating as—falling in love——

NANCY. You are—thorough.

(Goes to piano. MRS. WINSLOW *opens the dining-room door.)*

MRS. WINSLOW. *(Above* L. *of* T.L.C.*)* Richard, come to dinner. And kindly bring Martha's guest.

RICHARD. *(At* U.R. *of sofa)* I want you please to tell the family something! Tomorrow you can have the whole thing back. *(She enters, closing the door behind her.)*

MRS. WINSLOW. But—but—oh dear, and I thought I was through with my worries. With—with Oliver helping me I live in constant fear that when I pass on you won't all be provided for, as your Father wished.

RICHARD. Tell you what, Mother—divvy it up.

MRS. WINSLOW. Divvy it up?

RICHARD. Yes.

MRS. WINSLOW. *(Eagerly)* Can one?

RICHARD. Simple. Trust fund. Alan and me trustees.

MRS. WINSLOW. Oh—what a relief it would be! *(Going out into dining-room)* Children, Richard has found a very happy solution to our difficulties.

ALL. *(Off* L.*)* What's that, Mother? etc. . . .

MRS. WINSLOW. We are to divide things up—a trust fund—a—— *(Her voice is lost in the family's, except for* OLIVER'S *exclamations of refusal.)*

MARK *and* AUGUSTA. Good idea——

MUFF. That's the first sensible thing I've heard about money in this house for a month——

OLIVER. *(Through the above)* No, no! I won't stand by and see Mother forced into something——

ALL. *(From all)* Sit down—sit down, Oliver! *(Etc.* RICHARD *closes the door.)*

RICHARD. *(To L.L. of sofa)* Was that what you wanted?

NANCY. *(Extending her hand on him)* Good-bye and thanks a lot. You've been awfully illuminating. Now, whenever I think I'm being particularly noble, I'll know I'm just pinning roses on Nancy.

(WARN.)

RICHARD. I can't imagine anyone wearing her roses so well.

NANCY. Thanks—you needn't bother. *(She covers her face)* Oh—I'm in bits. *(Sits—lower end of sofa.)*

RICHARD. *(Sits on arm of sofa)* Nancy—dear, dear Nancy—listen to me—can you listen to me now? *(She looks up. He smiles)* 'Cause I knew that the gorgeous person who sailed in here like a ship never could, till her sails came down a little.

NANCY. I can't live this way. You've got to get them up again!

RICHARD. That wouldn't be hard—— Oh, Nancy, you *are* so lovely.

NANCY. *(Rising—to L. of C.2. Cynically)* Yes, I told you you needn't bother.

RICHARD. It's no bother.

NANCY. Anyway, it doesn't work.

RICHARD. *(Is front of sofa)* It would, if I could be with you right along and keep telling you what I really think of you.

NANCY. *(Going to him)* I—I don't suppose you'd be willing to marry me?

RICHARD. Yes, I would.

NANCY. *(Sits on front arm of the sofa)* Would you?

RICHARD. *(Sits on arm of sofa at L. of her)* I really would.

NANCY. You are sweet. *(They kiss.)* There, that works!—And Richard.

RICHARD. What?

(*RING.*)

NANCY. You are my equal.
RICHARD. I'll tell you something better than that.
NANCY. What?
RICHARD. You're mine!

CURTAIN

(*The curtain starts early very slowly, is about twelve feet from stage. "You're Mine!" Signal brings it down rest of distance.*)

ACT ONE—SCENE

The Winslow's living-room is a long, rectangular room which has served for years as the congregating place of the clan. The color scheme, so far as there is one, is blue and yellow, with ivory woodwork.

At back center there is a large fireplace, fender and grate.

And left side is nine feet six inches from return up. The C. is the center of a recess space that contains the door which swings on stage and up, the door to the dining-room.

A seven-foot piece joins this perpendicular on stage. The C. of this is the C. of the high French windows, which swing down stage, and leads into porch.

The back wall is three and a half feet above the window-piece. A curved bookcase sets into the curve, joining the two pieces.

The back wall proper is sixteen feet wide and thirteen feet from the setting line. The right side of stage is exactly the same as the left. The door in the R. side leads to the hall, general entrance, etc.

Through the French windows may be seen the side railing, pillars, awnings, etc., of the porch, which is paved with large green tiles. A green hedge runs up stage on both sides, from the up-stage end of the awning piece, another hedge runs off stage. A landscape drop at back. A set rock piece, covered with vines, carries off the ends of the drop.

Two trees are in front of the set rocks.

Interior backings for both doors.

Ceiling covers set.

Fireplace backing.

KEY FOR ACTS I AND III

Nos.

1 Library table
2 Bench
3 Armchair
4 Sofa
5 Wing armchair
6 Work-table
7
8
9 Windsor armchair
10 Baby grand piano
11 Chairs
12 Leather-backed chairs.
13 Rugs
14 Cabinets, half round
15 Standard
16 Picture, "Jabez Winslow"
17 Panels
18 Wall brackets
19 Fire-grate
20 Fender
21 Hearth-stone
22 Backing
23 Returns
24 Doors
25 Windows
26 Chair on porch
27 Bookcases
28 Backings, interior
29 Plan of awning
30
31 Pilaster
32 Column

33 Hedges
34 Set rocks
35 Drop
36 Set trees
37 Spotlight stands
38 The porch
39 Transparencies
40 Strips on floor

LIGHTING

Focusing

Baby Spots hanging in one, 250 watts, R.

Nos.

1—Amber, left side of hammock, Act II

2—Blue, Frost, window right center, Act II.

3—Amber, up center, Act I.

4—Flesh, upper end of sofa, Act I.

5—Blue, Frost—lantern right center and edge of shutter, Act II.

6—Two Blues, Frost, center of wall, Act II.

7—Amber, below lantern right center, silhouette, Act II.

8—Flesh, sitting chair above table left center, Act I.

9—Amber, sitting armchair right, Act I.

10—Flesh, no cut out, amber up center, Act I.

11—Amber, sitting chair above table left center, Act I.

12—Frost, Flesh, no cut-out, up center, Act I.

13—Amber, Frost, no cutout, mantel and rug, Act I.

14—Amber below lantern up left center, silhouette, Act II.

15—Frost, blue, trellis on left up high, Act II.

16—Flesh, Frost above piano, Act I.

17—Frost, blue on wall chair right center, Act II.

18—Amber sitting stool right center, Act I.

Stand lamps on R.:

Top

1—Frost, blue on corner up right vine, Act II.

2—Clear, hits top of awning on right, Act II.
3—Amber—chair center—Head, Act II.
4—Amber, chair center—Head, Act II.
5—Clear across stage, Act II.
6—Clear across stage, Act II.

Stand lamps on L.:

Top

1—Amber corner of backing up high on left, Act II.
2—Amber-stone right center, Head, Act I.
3—Amber, lower right, sofa-Head, Act I.
4—Amber, armchair center head, Act I.
5—Amber lower right of sofa. Head, Act I.
6—Straw on stage, Act II.

Transparencies:

Back of drop, above windows right and left. Sunset 2-30 lamp strips, 60 Watts. 3 circuits, Blue, Amber and Pink, Elevated, one shows through each window.

Furniture Properties:

A brown carpet covers the stage.
A large wing armchair is up right of center.
Small work-table at right of it.
High ladder-backed chair at left of mantel.
High ladder-backed chair at right of mantel.
Mantel up center.
Standard and shield at left of mantel.
Small side chair front of left of mantel.
Baby grand piano at right center, keyboard at R.
Small side chair at right of above.
Armchair, Windsor, front of piano.
Oval table, small, down right center.
Stool, oval, above.
Sofa at left center.
Table (Desk) at left of sofa, running off stage.
Armchair above table.
Bench front of table.

Cabinet, half-round, below door on right.
Cabinet, half round, below door on left.
Porch chair above the window on right on porch.
Two book-cases, filled, within curves of set up right center and left center.

Pictures:

Portrait of a man, old-fashioned, gold frame, "Jabez," hangs over the mantel.
Panel of flowers above door right.
Panel of flowers above door left.

Rugs:

Front of mantel, black, with roses.
Front of sofa, rose and green.
At left of piano, old gold.
At door left, brown and buff.

Curtains:

French window right.
One pair, sliding on rods, gray silk, at bottom of window.
One pair drop, on rods, gray silk, at top of window.
French windows left.
Same as above.
Door on right.
Valance figured black chintz.
Two side curtains figured black chintz.
Door on left.
Same as above.

Foliage:

Two trees stand in front of set piece up right.
Two trees stand in front of set piece up left.
Vines, etc., on set pieces.

Bells:

Four small hand-bells, to ring before curtain rises on each Act.

SMALL PROPS.

On Table left center:
Pad of onion skin paper.
Pencils.
Large check book, three checks to page.
Writing set: Blotter, pens, ink.
Rugs: Red roses, black at mantel, rose and green at sofa, old gold at piano, buff and brown at door left.
Two magazines.
Ash-tray, match holder.
Pocket-knife—Richard's.
Slate pencils.

On Sofa left center:
Four cushions.
"Atlantic Monthly."

Pictures:
Portrait, gold frame, over mantel, panel flowers, above the doors right and left.

Wall Brackets:
Two below doors right and left.

On Oval Table down right center:
Picture scrap book.

On Armchair right:
Straw hat—Mark's. Hat band.

On Work-Table up right center:
Box of chocolates.

Work-Box:
Round piece of lace.
White cloth.
Needles.
White thread.
Thimble.
Scissors.

At Mantel up C.:
Fender, brass, grate.

Off Stage up left:
Puppy.
Kitten.
Off Stage R.:
Three newspapers.
One newspaper.
Manuscript, blue cover.
Door-bell.
Dog bark.
On Mantel:
Clock, black marble.
Two vases, China.
Two square urns of flowers.
Ash-tray match-holder.
On Piano right:
Two oil lamps.
Vase of Roses.
Two magazines.
Sheet music.
Personal:
Pipe, Richard.
Tobacco-pouch, tobacco, Richard.
Matches, Richard.
Silk handkerchief, Richard.
Key to room, Richard.
Pocket knife, Oliver.
Cigarette case, filled, Mark.
Coin, Mark.
Pocket mirror, Mark.
Fountain-pen, Oliver.
On Porch up right:
Chair.
Law-book.
On Cabinets right and left:
Candelabrum, three candles.

Foots:
Blue, 'way down.

White and amber, one-eighth up.
Pink, one-quarter up.

X-ray:
Blue, pink and amber, up full.

Baby spots hanging in one:
Nos. 3, 4, 8, 9, 10, 11, 12, 16, 17, 18, up full.
Act II, one-half up.

Entrance lights:
At doors left and right.
Four-lamp strips—2 frost blue, 1 amber, 1 pink.

Spots on stage:
On left—1000 Watt, amber, on foliage of hedge.
On right—1000 Watt, amber, on foliage, stand center of stage.

House Border:
Border No. 4, Amber one-half, one-half up.
Blue, up full.

Stand on right:
Nos. 1, 3, 4, up full.

Stand on left:
Nos. 2, 3, 4, 5, up full.

Transparency:
Right and left, up full.

Strips on floor up right and left behind hedges back of windows right and left:
Four light blues, up full.

Wall brackets:
Right and left, not lighted.

KEY FOR ACT II

Nos.
1—Passageway to garden.
2—Plan of plank.
3—Railing.
4—Hedges.
5—Hedges.
6—Pilaster.
7—Columns.
8—Windows.
9—Doors.
10—Hanging tabs.
11—Book-cases.
12—Exterior backings, porch.
13—Interior backings.
14—Hammock, swing.
15—Smoking-table.
16—Stool.
17—Table.
18—Side chairs.
19—Windsor chairs (arm).
20—Armchairs, rush-bottom.
21—Seat, table-top, back.
22—Side chairs.
23—Lanterns.
24—Trees.
25—False proscenium.
26—The Living-room.

LIGHTING

Act II

Foots:
Blue, up full.
White and amber, up full.
Pink, up one-half.
X-Ray left:
Blue-Pink-Amber, up full.
Baby spots hanging in one:
Everything (18), up full.
Stand Side Lamps:
Everything right and left, up full.
Spots and Open Lamps on left:
Two 1000 Watts, amber, on speaker stand.
Open Lamps:
No. 1—three-quarters light blue—broken.
One-quarter clear.
Stands at edge of hedge, tipped, and through window up left center.
No. 2—One-third light blue.
Two-thirds amber.
Stand high on stand.
Hits trellis.
No 3—One-third amber.
Two-thirds clear.
Stands high on stand.
Hits gateway to garden on left.
Spots and open lamps on right:
One 1000 Watt Spot, amber.
Hits vine on backing, high up.
One Flood lamp, one-half clear.
Stand high on stand.
Hits over top of awning on right.
House Border No. 4:
Blue circuit, up full.

White, one-quarter up.
Amber, up one-eighth.

Scene:

The Porch. It is moderately deep and the back wall is the reverse of the living-room back wall, with the French windows on either side, swinging up stage, showing part of the living-room. The porch floor is of green tiles. Blue and white awnings on right and left sides.

The Awning sections on left and right. It is 14 feet 6 inches from the setting line to the French window, or house. On setting line is a large round pillar; a railing, boarded in, 8 feet 6 inches long; from the pillar up stage an opening 4 feet wide leads off to the lawn; a pilaster at the upper end against the house. The awning is attached to the rafter between the pillar and the pilaster. The house extends off stage from the pilaster about 12 feet and a wing breaks down the mask. A trellis is painted on the pilaster piece. A green hedge is back of railings and another, higher, runs off stage from the pillars. Both sides, right and left, are same.

The side pieces of Act I continuing the doors are moved up stage, forming the side walls of the living-room, the doors swing onward up stage. The windows are backed by tabs hanging at the upper ends of the above pieces and wide enough for the purpose.

Border is in one, about eighteen inches, deep scalloped—represents the edge of the awning. Ceiling over porch, same as Act I.

PROPERTIES

Furniture:

Ground cloth, green tiles, covers the stage.
Hammock, swings on low standards, center.
Stool in front.

Smoking-table (higher stool) at right of hammock.
Oval table, double gate-leg, at left center.
Wooden chair above it.
Wooden chair at left of it.
Wooden chair at right of it.
A table for the speaker at the railing on left.
Armchair, Windsor, down right center 1.
Bench with table-top back at railing, on right.
Armchair, high back, rush bottom, up left center.
Armchair, high back, rush bottom, up right center.
Armchair.

In house:

A flat bookcase stands front at tab, above the door right, with the small chair of Act I front of it.
Same back of door left.

Foliage:

A branch on the pillar down left for shadows.
Tree at left for shadows.
Two trees at backings on left.
Tree on right.
Large vine on backing on right.
Vines on trellis on right and left.

SMALL PROPS.

On Hammock center:

Two—cushions.
Four—balloons on right side.

On Table left center:

Italian pitcher.
Speech in pitcher.
Ash-tray match-holder.
Newspaper.
Two magazines.
Two books.

On Hedge left:

Two Flag-Holders.

On high stool right of H.:
Ash-tray match-holder.
Cigarette humidor.
Pipe on sky-rockets right and left.
Balloons, colored, on lanterns.
Two law books on armchair up right center.
Off Stage up C.:
Breakfast tray, dishes, napkin, grapefruit, toast, etc.
Tray:
Pitcher of ice water, four glasses.
Bundle of American flags.
Two American flags, silk, rolled up.
Three Roman candles.
Four campchairs.
Cup of coffee.
Manicuring set.
Off stage I:
Brass Band.
Clappers.
Tin Horns.
Cowbells.
Shot pad.
Personal:
Pipe, tobacco, matches—Richard.
Cigarette-case, filled—Mark.
Will, old—Alan.

LIGHTING

ACT III

Foots:
Blue, way down.
White and amber, one-eighth up.
Pink, one-quarter up.

X-Ray:
Blue, pink and amber—up full.
Baby Spots hanging in one:
Nos. 3, 4, 8, 9, 10; Nos. 11, 12, 13, 16, 18—Up Full.
Entrance Lights:
At doors left and right.
Four-lamp strips—2 frost blue, 1 amber, 1 pink.
Spots up stage:
On left, 1000 Watt, amber, on foliage of hedge.
On right, 1000 Watt, amber, on foliage, stands center of stage.
House Border:
Border No. 4—Amber one-half—one-half up. Blue up full.
Stand on right:
Nos. 1, 3, 4—Up Full.
Stand on left:
Nos. 2, 3, 4, 5—Up Full.
Transparency:
Right and left—Up Full.
Strips on floor up right and left:
Four-light blues.
Wall Brackets:
Right and left, not lighted.

PROPS.

Act III

On Table left center:
Writing set.
Blotter.
Pen.
Ink.
Large checkbook, Act I.
Ash-tray match-holder at left.
Magazines
Books.

Envelope with letter in it.
Postage stamp in drawer.
Pencils.
Paper.

On Sofa left center:

Four cushions.

Clock on mantel stopped at five-twenty.

On Work-table up right center:

Work-box.

On Piano:

Music.
Vase of flowers, front.
Two law books, Act I, center.
Lamp (upper end).
Magazine.

Off stage up right:

Puppy.

Off stage up center:

Top bell for striking.

Personal:

Pipe, etc.—Richard.
Fountain-pen—Mark.
Legal paper—Oliver.